New Covenant Living

Released to Live by the Spirit

By
Kurt Litwiller

Live in a covenant relationship with Jesus!

Kurt

New Covenant Living

Copyright © 2010 by Kurt Litwiller

All rights reserved. No part of this book may be used, reproduced, stored in a retrieval system, or transmitted in any form whatsoever — including electronic, photocopy, recording — without prior written permission from the author, except in the case of brief quotations embodied in critical articles or reviews.

All Scripture quotations, unless otherwise indicated, are taken from the *Holy Bible, New International Version®. NIV®.* Copyright © 1973, 1978, 1984 by International Bible Society. Used by permission of Zondervan. All rights reserved.

Edited by Janelle Litwiller and Michael Milligan

FIRST EDITION

ISBN 9780982657423

Library of Congress Control Number: 2010923809

Published by
NewBookPublishing.com, a division of Reliance Media, Inc.
2395 Apopka Blvd., #200, Apopka, FL 32703
NewBookPublishing.com

Printed in the United States of America

Dedication

This book is dedicated first and foremost to my Lord and Savior Jesus Christ who loved me enough to die in my place. No words can describe the joy I have in the freedom He provides. I would also like to dedicate this book to my church family at Boynton Mennonite Church. Thank you for your love, support, encouragement, and most of all your friendship. I am honored to serve the Lord Jesus Christ side by side with you. And finally I dedicate this to my wife Janelle. You are my faithful partner on this journey of faith. Thank you for walking with me and helping me along the way. Thanks again for the many hours you spent editing this book for me. May God

New Covenant Living

Table Of Contents

INTRODUCTION 7

   1. New Covenant Promised 11

   2. Law Fulfilled 19

   3. Temporary Purpose 29

   4. Living Under One Covenant 39

   5. Accepting Our Inheritance 47

   6. The New Commandments 55

   7. Approaching God 61

   8. A Covenant Sign 69

   9. Judged by Law? 79

   10. Sacred Days in the Church 87

   11. Living Under the New Covenant 101

CONCLUSION 111

ABOUT THE AUTHOR 116

Introduction

Many Christians are divided on how we are to view the two main covenants that are in the Bible—one is from the Old Testament and the other is from the New Testament. Are we under both the new and old covenants, or are we just under the new covenant that Jesus ushered in? You look at verses like Matthew 5:17-18, *"Do not think that I have come to abolish the Law or the Prophets; I have not come to abolish them but to fulfill them. I tell you the truth, until heaven and earth disappear, not the smallest letter, not the least stroke of a pen, will by any means disappear from the Law until everything is accomplished."* After reading a verse like that, you probably think, "We are definitely under both covenants." However, if you continue to read in the New Testament, you read the words found in *Galatians 5:18, "But if you are led by the Spirit, you are not under law."* This verse seems to be saying that we are just under the new covenant—we are no longer under the law. So which is it?

This was a question that I came head to head with several years ago. I was a pastor for five years before I had my eyes opened to the depth of this topic. First, let me tell you that I was raised in a strong Christian family. We were at church three times a week. We went Sunday morning, Sunday night, and again on Wednesday night for youth group. I couldn't get out of going to church even if I wanted to. My parents modeled the Christian life by having family devotions every night. We learned the way of God.

After five years of pastoring at my church, I felt like my spirit needed to be fed more. So I tried to find a place to worship where I was not actually in charge of the events of the service. This was difficult because most churches meet on Sunday morning, just like mine. I found a place to worship on Saturday, at The Seventh Day Adventist Church. I did not know at this point the struggles and learning that would come out of the several months that I spent there.

The Seventh Day Adventists really dig into the Word of God. I respect them greatly for that! It really encouraged me to see that people in the church truly knew the Bible. They really teach their church to dig into the Bible for themselves. I was enjoying studying the Bible with them, and I was also enjoying their ability to stretch me in some of my own beliefs. Then it happened. They gave me a book to read that turned my world upside down. This book talked about how the American church only keeps nine out of the Ten Commandments. The commandment the church doesn't follow according to the book was "Remember the Sabbath day by keeping it holy." The book goes on to explain how the Sabbath starts after sunset on Friday night and goes until sunset on Saturday.

As I read this book, it made a lot of sense to me. I believed that we were not keeping the Sabbath Day. I grew up in a Christian home that stressed the importance of following the Ten Commandments, and I felt anguished that I wasn't keeping one of them. I didn't want to do nine out of ten things that God wanted me to do— I wanted to completely follow Him. Who changed the Sabbath to Sunday? I don't see anyone in scripture saying, "You can move the Sabbath Day to Sunday now."

Again, let me remind you that I had been a pastor at this church for the past five years. I went to the church board, and told them that I was struggling with this issue. I couldn't make sense of this, and it was really ripping me apart to think that I was not keeping one of God's commandments. After a few months of discussion with my church board, I was close to resigning as pastor, because I felt convicted that the Sabbath was Friday & Saturday. I could not continue to teach at the Mennonite Church on Sunday, if I thought it was wrong. I didn't want to lead them down a path that I thought was wrong.

Then one day, one of the board members sent me the link to a website and told me to check it out. I went to the website and I had a huge paradigm shift in my thinking. I now look at the Ten Commandments and the law completely different than I used too. It was then that I realized that I was supposed to be living under the new covenant with Jesus Christ. For those who disagree with me, please read on and see what you think.

Covenant was a term that I was not very familiar with. I heard it several times but I could not tell you what it meant. Covenant simply means an agreement between two parties. Your marriage relationship is a covenant relationship. Both husband and wife stand before God and make a covenant vow before Him. You agree that you will love, honor, and be faithful to the other person so long as you both shall live. The covenant relationship is a very special relationship. My relationship with my neighbor is not a covenant relationship. I have a great relationship with my neighbor, but I don't have a committed relationship with him like I do with my wife.

The covenant relationship requires two parties to

fulfill their part of an agreement. We are called to be in a covenant relationship with God. In order to live out that relationship, we must first understand whether we are living under the new covenant or under both covenants at the same time.

Chapter One

New Covenant Promised

The history of the Israelites was a roller coaster ride. They would follow God for a while, and then they would turn their backs on Him. Through the Israelites, we see the true image of humanity—serving God and then straying away because of the things of the world.

We will start our study with the Israelites as they were in slavery in Egypt for 430 years. God called Moses to bring His people out of slavery and to lead them to the Promise Land. On the way to the Promise Land, they spent 40 years in the desert because of their unbelief. It was in the desert that God made a covenant with Israel. The covenant we know today as the old covenant—the law found in the Old Testament.

Let's take a closer look at the covenant stipulations that God made with the people of Israel in the Old Testament. Moses said to the people in Deuteronomy 4:13, *"He declared to you his covenant, the Ten Commandments, which he commanded you to follow and then wrote them on two stone tablets."* Israel's part of the covenant was to keep the Ten Commandments, but that was not the only thing. Moses teaches them more of what God says all through the first five books of the Old Testament…and in Deuteronomy 29:1 it says, *"These are the terms of the covenant the Lord commanded Moses to make with the Israelites in Moab, <u>in addition</u> to the covenant he had made with them at Horeb."* So Moses gave them many more teachings of God besides the Ten Commandments that they were to follow—such as dietary laws (what they could eat and not eat), sacrificial laws (animal sacrifices that they had to perform to please God), and civil laws. This was Israel's part of the covenant; this is what they had to follow. God's part of the covenant (what He agreed to) was to lead them into the Promise Land which flowed with milk and honey. God was going to provide them with a land that was filled with the best of everything. If Israel kept their part of the covenant, God was going to provide them with His protection and blessings. Israel is excited about living in this great Promise Land with the best of everything and knowing God is watching over them. Their response to the covenant God was making with them was, *"We will do everything the LORD has said; we will obey."*[1] They accepted the terms of this covenant, but we know that Israel doesn't fulfill what they agreed to do. They turn their backs on God and they chase after other idols in their lives.

God saw their unfaithfulness to what they claimed they would live out. In Jeremiah 11:10 God says, *"They have returned to the sins of their forefathers, who refused to listen to my words. They have followed other gods to serve them. Both the house of Israel and the house of Judah have <u>broken the covenant</u> I made with their forefathers."* Both Israel & Judah broke their part of the agreement. We see that God is not happy that they have chosen to break the agreement that they had made with Him. No one would be happy if someone was unfaithful to them in an agreement that was made. Jeremiah goes on and paints a vivid picture for us to see God's displeasure. In Jeremiah 18, God tells Jeremiah to go to the house of the potter. So Jeremiah goes to the potter's house and he sees the potter at the wheel forming a pot out of clay. The potter takes great care in making the pot. The message is that the people of Israel are the clay and God is the potter shaping them as He sees fit. It is important for us to see that Israel is the pot, because in the very next chapter, Jeremiah 19, God has Jeremiah take the clay pot and smash it. Israel's disobedience to their covenant with God left them broken. Israel is sent into exile where they are prisoners of other countries for 70 years. All seemed lost.

But in the midst of the exile, they get some good news. We have all heard Jeremiah 29:11, *"'For I know the plans I have for you,' declares the Lord, 'plans to prosper you and not to harm you, plans to give you hope and a future.'"* Even though they were unfaithful to God and they broke His covenant and were prisoners in a foreign land, there is still a promise of something good. What can be good when their relationship with God had been severed? What good could be promised? God promised to restore them back to Him. God knew the old covenant couldn't work, because no man can live up to their part. So God promises a new covenant; a new agreement between God and man. In Jeremiah 31:31-33 we see this new covenant that God promises to give in the future,

> [31] *"The time is coming,"* declares the LORD,
> *"when I will make a new covenant*
> *with the house of Israel*
> *and with the house of Judah.*
> [32] *It will not be like the covenant*
> *I made with their forefathers*

> when I took them by the hand
>> to lead them out of Egypt,
> because they broke my covenant,
>> though I was a husband to them,"
> declares the LORD.
> [33] "This is the covenant I will make with the
>> house of Israel
> after that time," declares the LORD.
>> "I will put my law in their minds
>> and write it on their hearts.
>> I will be their God,
>> and they will be my people.
> [34] No longer will a man teach his neighbor,
>> or a man his brother, saying, 'Know the
>> LORD,'
> because they will all know me,
>> from the least of them to the greatest,"
>> declares the LORD.
>> "For I will forgive their wickedness
>> and will remember their sins no more."

God promises Israel a new covenant. It will not be like the one that He made with their forefathers when He brought them out of Egypt. It will not be based on the written law, but the law would be written on their hearts and minds.

There was a problem with the first covenant. God needed to establish a new covenant (or agreement) because if one party broke that agreement, the covenant was broken. The new covenant that was promised would be superior to the old covenant law. Hebrews 8:6-7 says, "But the ministry Jesus has received is as superior to *theirs as the covenant of which he is mediator is superior to the old one, and it is founded on better promises. For if there had been nothing wrong with that first covenant, no place would have been sought for another."* Something went wrong with the first covenant. There was nothing wrong with the law, but the problem was that man was unable to live up to their part of the covenant agreement. People lacked the power to obey the law. There is no way anyone could keep their covenant agreement with God under the old covenant. No one can follow the whole law. Romans 3:23 says, *"for all have sinned and fall short of the glory of God."* We know we are all sinners because each one of us has broken God's perfect standard that He set up for us. For people who still want to live under the law, James 2:10 says, *"For whoever keeps the whole law and yet stumbles at just one point is guilty of breaking all of it."* Who has never done anything contrary to the law? If we were judged by the law, we would be in trouble. We are just like Israel—we can't keep the old covenant law.

    So God sent His one and only Son into the world to establish this new covenant with all the nations of the world, not just the Jewish people. Jesus says in Luke 22:20, *"...This cup is the new covenant in my blood, which is poured out for you."* Jesus' blood ushered in the new covenant with God. God spoke to us through His prophets, but there was no way we could grasp the message that He had for us. So God had to become one of us to show us the way.

    I heard a story once that can help open our eyes to God's reason for coming to earth to save us. There was a woman who was going to a Christmas Eve service, and she asked her husband if he wanted to go. Her husband, being an unbeliever, did not want to go along with her. He told her, "How can you believe in all that foolishness—God would become a man? There is no way that would happen." So the woman loaded up her children in the car and headed to the church for the service. Not too long after she left, a blizzard blew in. The man looked out the window, but could not see more than 2 feet in front of him because of the white out conditions. The man sat before the fire and started to read. All of a sudden he heard a thump on the window. He went over to check it out, but he could not see anything through the wintery conditions. He sat down again and he heard another thump on the window. He got up and checked it out, but there was nothing there that he could see. He decided to go outside and see if he could see what was going on. When he went out, he saw that there was a flock of geese caught in the blizzard, and flying around in his yard. He felt sorry for the geese, so he opened up his barn door, but they did not fly in. He went around to the other side of them and tried to herd them into the barn, but they just scattered. He went inside and got bread crumbs and left a trail to the barn, but the geese did not go after the food. He could not think of anything else to do. He thought to himself, "If only I was a goose, I could show them the way." Then he thought of the goose he had in his barn. He went and got his goose and walked around the flock of geese. He let go of his goose and his goose made a direct path back to the warm barn. The rest of the geese followed his goose to the warm shelter of the barn. As the man thought about what happened that night, he realized that it was exactly the same thing that God did for us. God tried to bring us into safety. He gave us His law, He sent us His prophets…but we were like the geese and did not follow. So God sent His only Son, Jesus, to become one of us to show us the way.

There is no other way to get to God other than through the new covenant sacrifice of Jesus Christ. Jesus says in John 14:6, *"I am the way and the truth and the life. No one comes to the Father except through me."* It is impossible to get to God through the old covenant law by trying to live a good life. A pleasing relationship with God only comes through Jesus Christ.

Jesus became one of us to save us from the curse of the law. The curse for the law breaker is eternal punishment in hell. God has a new way of relating with man. Hebrews 8:13 says, *"By calling this covenant 'new,' he has made the first one obsolete; and what is obsolete and aging will soon disappear."* The first covenant has been made obsolete. The law cannot save us from our sins, it just reveals our sinfulness. It is now through the new covenant, the blood of Jesus, that we can be pleasing in His sight. There is no way that we can be righteous under the old covenant.

Jeremiah 3 talks about Israel's unfaithfulness to God and how God was grieved about the old covenant. In verse 8, God says, *"I gave faithless Israel her certificate of divorce and sent her away because of all her adulteries. Yet I saw that her unfaithful sister Judah had no fear; she also went out and committed adultery."* Both houses of Israel went astray, and were unfaithful to God. They broke the covenant and worshiped other gods. God was angry with His people and was calling them to come back to Him. There is a great promise in Jeremiah 3 that goes along with the new covenant. In verse 16 it says, *"'In those days, when your numbers have increased greatly in the land,' declares the LORD, 'men will no longer say, The ark of the covenant of the LORD. It will never enter their minds or be remembered; it will not be missed, nor will another one be made.'"* We know from the context of this verse, that this verse is pointing to the coming of the Messiah. In the Old Testament, the Ark of the Covenant represented God's presence. But when the Messiah comes, no one will miss the ark because the presence of God is in their midst through Jesus.

The Ark of the Covenant was the heart of the old covenant. Inside the ark were the Ten Commandments. God says in Jeremiah that *"The ark will never enter their minds or be remembered; it will not be missed, nor will another one be made."* There will be no need for the ark after Jesus comes—there will be no need for the law that is inside. Remember what God said in Jeremiah 31:33-34 when he was talking about the coming of the new covenant. *"'...I will put my law in their minds and write it on their hearts. I will be their God, and they will be my people. No longer will a man teach his neighbor, or a man his brother, saying, 'Know the LORD,' because they will all know me, from the least of them to the greatest,' declares the LORD..."* God is going to write the law on our hearts so that it will govern our everyday lives. We don't need to ask our brother to teach us the law, because we have the Holy Spirit inside of us teaching us the truth. The law abiding presence of God that once was in the ark, is now in our hearts and minds through the Holy Spirit.

As you read on in this book, you will definitely see that the new covenant is "superior" to the old covenant in many ways. For the old covenant was written on stone with no power to help us, while the new covenant is written on our hearts by the Holy Spirit, which gives us the power to live obedient lives for our God.

Chapter 2

Law Fulfilled

In the last chapter, we saw how God promised us a new covenant through His Son Jesus Christ. So when Jesus came to earth and spoke to the people, He told them what ushering in this new covenant does with the old covenant (law). Jesus said in Matthew 5,

> [17] "Do not think that I have come to abolish the Law or the Prophets; I have not come to abolish them but to fulfill them. [18] I tell you the truth, until heaven and earth disappear, not the smallest letter, not the least stroke of a pen, will by any means disappear from the Law until everything is accomplished. [19] Anyone who breaks one of the least of these commandments and teaches others to do the same will be called least in the kingdom of heaven, but whoever practices and teaches these commands will be called great in the kingdom of heaven. [20] For I tell you that unless your righteousness surpasses that of the Pharisees and the teachers of the law, you will certainly not enter the kingdom of heaven.

All Christians believe that Jesus came to fulfill the law. No one can deny that fact because it is plainly stated in scripture. The difference of agreement comes in asking how much of the law did Jesus come to fulfill? In this chapter we will look a little closer at the four different parts of the Old Testament Law: Sacrificial/Ceremonial Law, Dietary Law, Civil Law, and Moral Law (Ten Commandments). Which of these did Jesus fulfill by dying upon the cross? I think we will come to realize that Jesus' sacrifice on the cross fulfilled the entire law.

Sacrificial/Ceremonial Law

The Israelites were required by the law to offer sacrifices to the Lord. There were other sacrifices as well, which were written in the law and were voluntary acts of worship. The different sacrifices that they brought before God were: burnt offerings, grain offerings, fellowship offerings, sin offerings, and guilt offerings. "The burnt offerings were a voluntary act of worship, atonement for unintentional sin in general, and expression of devotion, commitment and complete surrender to God. The grain offerings were also voluntary acts of worship, recognition of God's goodness and provision, and devotion to God. Fellowship offerings were also a voluntary act of worship, as well as thanksgiving and fellowship (it included a communal meal). The sin offering was a mandatory act of atonement for specific unintentional sins, confession of sin, forgiveness of sin, and cleansing from defilement. The guilt offerings were also mandatory atonement for unintentional sin requiring restitution, cleansing from defilement, making restitution, and paying a 20% fine."[2] These sacrifices were part of the law in the old covenant.

There were also many different ceremonies Israel

had to observe: "The Sabbath, the Sabbath Year, Year of Jubilee, Passover, Unleavened Bread, Firstfruits, Weeks, Trumpets, Day of Atonement, Tabernacles, Sacred Assembly, and Purim."[3] The Israelites had to observe these days according to the Law.

There is no dispute among Christians that Jesus completely fulfilled the sacrificial law. The New Testament is filled with verses showing that Jesus' blood was the sacrifice for our sins. The author of Hebrews used this as a central theme of his letter. *Hebrews 9:11-12 says, "When Christ came as high priest of the good things that are already here, he went through the greater and more perfect tabernacle that is not man-made, that is to say, not a part of this creation. He did not enter by means of the blood of goats and calves; but he entered the Most Holy Place once for all by his own blood, having obtained eternal redemption."* "The way into the sanctuary of God's presence was closed to the people under the former covenant because the blood of animal sacrifices could never completely atone for their sins. Now, however, believers can come to the throne of grace since the Perfect Priest has offered the Perfect Sacrifice, atoning for sin once for all."[4] Jesus' death on the cross purchased our eternal redemption so we don't have to sacrifice animals year after year.

There is also a large consensus that Jesus fulfilled the ceremonial part of the law as well. As Christians we do not have to set up feasts to remember the Passover, Sabbath, Sabbath Year, etc. *Colossians 2:16-17, "Therefore do not let anyone judge you by what you eat or drink, or with regard to a religious festival, a New Moon celebration or a Sabbath day. These are a shadow of the things that were to come; the reality, however, is found in Christ."* All of these ceremonies were a shadow of the true revelation we find in Christ Jesus. I haven't seen a Christian yet celebrate the Sabbath year or the Passover feast with their family.[5] It seems clear to most Christians that Jesus fulfilled the sacrificial/ceremonial law.

Dietary Law

The Israelites were required by the law to abstain from certain foods. For example, in verses 3 and 4 of Leviticus chapter 11, the Lord told the Israelites that the land animals that they could eat had to have two specific things: a split hoof completely divided and it had to chew its cud. In verses 9-12, God says that the Israelites could also eat any creatures living in the water of the seas and the streams that had fins and scales, but in verses 13-19 they couldn't eat certain types of birds, such as: the eagle, the vulture, the black vulture, the red kite, any kind of black kite, any kind of raven, the horned owl, the screech owl, the gull, any kind of hawk, the little owl, the cormorant, the great owl, the white owl, the desert owl, the osprey, the stork, any kind of heron, the hoopoe and the bat. If you want to see any more of the foods that were unclean for them, read Leviticus 11.

Most mainline Christians believe that Christ fulfilled this part of the law as well.[6] We read what Jesus says in *Mark 7:19, "'For it doesn't go into his heart but into his stomach, and then out of his body.' (In saying this, Jesus declared all foods 'clean.')"* And also in Romans 14, Paul gives a whole chapter declaring all foods clean for Christians to eat. *Romans 14:14, 20 says, "As one who is in the Lord Jesus, I am fully convinced that no food is unclean in itself. But if anyone regards something as unclean, then for him it is unclean...Do not destroy the work of God for the sake of food. All food is clean, but it is wrong for a man to eat anything that causes someone else to stumble."* These verses show good evidence that Jesus' death on the cross fulfilled the dietary law.

Civil Law

Civil Laws are the laws that govern how we deal with one another. We don't talk much about these laws in our churches today, but there is no doubt that we all believe that these are fulfilled. *Exodus 21:17 says, "Anyone who curses his father or mother must be put to death."* If we followed this rule alone, we wouldn't have anyone making it out of their teenage years! We do not kill a child for talking back to their parents. You can also read all of Exodus 21 where it relays numerous laws about what you are to do in different situations. It is all about retribution to the person who harmed you. But Jesus makes it clear in Matthew 5:38-42 that we are not to use the law to get back at people who have wronged us. *"You have heard that it was said, 'Eye for eye, and tooth for tooth.' But I tell you, Do not resist an evil person. If someone strikes you on the right cheek, turn to him the other also. And if someone wants to sue you and take your tunic, let him have your cloak as well. If someone forces you to go one mile, go with him two miles. Give to the one who asks you, and do not turn away from the one who wants to borrow from you."* "Eye for eye, and tooth for tooth" was the old covenant way of handling disagreements. Jesus says in the new covenant we are to turn the other cheek. If Jesus was saying nothing changes in the new covenant civil laws, He would have said something like this: "Resist an evil person. If someone strikes you on the right cheek, you have every right to strike him back. And if someone wants to sue you and take your tunic, sue him for his tunic and his cloak as well. If someone forces you to go one mile, just go with them one mile. Give to those who can give back to you, and make sure that they have the means to pay you back."(Kurt Litwiller Version) It is clear that Jesus did not want us to hold on to the old covenant civil laws.

For those who think we are still under the civil laws of the old covenant, do you believe this next verse is practiced often in our churches today? *Deuteronomy 25:5, "If brothers are living together and one of them dies without a son, his widow must not marry outside the family. Her husband's brother shall take her and marry her and fulfill the duty of a brother-in-law to her."* I can't imagine someone in the American church thinking that this law is binding for them. So it seems to me that Jesus came to fulfill the old covenant civil laws so that we are not required to follow them.

Moral Law

Moral Law is where Christians seem to disagree the most. Many people say that the Ten Commandments are the only part of the law that we are still supposed to follow today. They were written in stone and therefore we are still under the Moral law. I would have been one of these people the first five years of my pastoral ministry. The New Testament gives us a much different picture. 2 Corinthians 3 says,

> *[4] Such confidence as this is ours through Christ before God. [5] Not that we are competent in ourselves to claim anything for ourselves, but our competence comes from God. [6] He has made us competent as ministers*

of a new covenant—not of the letter but of the Spirit; for the letter kills, but the Spirit gives life.

⁷ Now if the ministry that brought death, which was engraved in letters on stone, came with glory, so that the Israelites could not look steadily at the face of Moses because of its glory, fading though it was, ⁸ will not the ministry of the Spirit be even more glorious? ⁹ If the ministry that condemns men is glorious, how much more glorious is the ministry that brings righteousness! ¹⁰ For what was glorious has no glory now in comparison with the surpassing glory. ¹¹ And if what was fading away came with glory, how much greater is the glory of that which lasts!

¹² Therefore, since we have such a hope, we are very bold. ¹³ We are not like Moses, who would put a veil over his face to keep the Israelites from gazing at it while the radiance was fading away. ¹⁴ But their minds were made dull, for to this day the same veil remains when the old covenant is read. It has not been removed, because only in Christ is it taken away. ¹⁵ Even to this day when Moses is read, a veil covers their hearts. ¹⁶ But whenever anyone turns to the Lord, the veil is taken away. ¹⁷ Now

> the Lord is the Spirit, and where the Spirit of the Lord is, there is freedom. [18] And we, who with unveiled faces all reflect the Lord's glory, are being transformed into his likeness with ever-increasing glory, which comes from the Lord, who is the Spirit.

In these verses, Paul was talking about the superiority of his calling in the new covenant. Paul is clearly pointing to the Ten Commandments in these verses. We know that because it says in verse 7, *"engraved in letters on stone"*. Paul references the story in Exodus 34 when Moses came down from the mountain with his face glowing. Moses met with the Lord, and his face glowed because of the glory of the Lord. He showed himself to the people of Israel and they were encouraged by seeing Moses' face. They knew that he had talked with the Lord. But in time, Moses' face stopped glowing and that was discouraging for the people. They would wonder, "Is God still with us?" So every time Moses met with God, he came down and showed the people his glowing face and told them what God had to say. Then he would put a veil over his face so that the Israelites could not see the glory fade from his face. This passage in 2 Corinthians says that there is a veil over people's hearts because they can't see the fading glory of the old covenant (which includes the 10 Commandments).

Verse 10-11 says, *"For what was glorious has no glory now in comparison with the surpassing glory. And if what was fading away came with glory, how much greater is the glory of that which lasts!"* Paul admits the law was glorious—the Ten Commandments were glorious. However, Paul goes on to say that this glory has no glory now and that it is fading away—compared to the surpassing glory in the new covenant that will never fade away.

Take a look at the comparisons between the two covenants:

OLD COVENANT	NEW COVENANT
Brought death & condemnation	Brings life & righteousness
Letter	Spirit
Engraved in stone	Written on our hearts
Fading glory	More, surpassing, lasting glory

Paul also says in Ephesians 2:14-18, *"For he himself is our peace, who has made the two one and has destroyed the barrier, the dividing wall of hostility, by abolishing in his flesh the law with its commandments and regulations. His purpose was to create in himself one new man out of the two, thus making peace, and in this one body to reconcile both of them to God through the cross, by which he put to death their hostility. He came and preached peace to you who were far away and peace to those who were near. For through him we both have access to the Father by one Spirit."* The law is what separated the Jews from the Gentiles. The Jews were set apart as God's people because God made this covenant with them and gave them the law to follow. Jesus came to *"abolish in his flesh the law with its commandments and regulations"* so that the Gentiles can become one with the Jews.

Paul also says in Colossians 2:13-14, *"When*

you were dead in your sins and in the uncircumcision of your sinful nature, God made you alive with Christ. He forgave us all our sins, having canceled the written code, with its regulations, that was against us and that stood opposed to us; he took it away, nailing it to the cross." The written code and all of its regulations that were nailed to the cross was the law that God gave to the people through Moses. The law stood opposed to us because everyone according to the law deserves eternal punishment.

As you read on, you will see that the Ten Commandments were fulfilled through Christ in other scriptures as well. Before I go any further, I want to make sure people understand that I am not "anti The Ten Commandments." I still believe that we live out the Ten Commandments, but that we do it through the new covenant relationship that we have in Christ. God's Spirit inside of us compels us to keep the true intention of the law, not just the law that is written in letters. He has freed us to serve Him with the attitude of our hearts, as well as our outward actions.

Chapter 3

Temporary Purpose

We now know that Jesus came to fulfill the law. Next, we are going to see the purpose of the law. Galatians 3 shows us the intention of the law.

> *[15] Brothers, let me take an example from everyday life. Just as no one can set aside or add to a human covenant that has been duly established, so it is in this case. [16] The promises were spoken to Abraham and to his seed. The Scripture does not say "and to seeds," meaning many people, but "and to your seed," meaning one person, who is Christ. [17] What I mean is this: The law, introduced 430 years later, does not set aside the covenant previously established by God and thus do away with the promise. [18] For if the inheritance depends on the law, then it no longer depends on a promise; but God in his grace gave it to Abraham through a promise.*
>
> *[19] What, then, was the purpose of the law? It was added because of transgressions until the Seed to*

whom the promise referred had come. The law was put into effect through angels by a mediator. ^{20} *A mediator, however, does not represent just one party; but God is one.* ^{21} *Is the law, therefore, opposed to the promises of God? Absolutely not! For if a law had been given that could impart life, then righteousness would certainly have come by the law.* ^{22} *But the Scripture declares that the whole world is a prisoner of sin, so that what was promised, being given through faith in Jesus Christ, might be given to those who believe.* ^{23} *Before this faith came, we were held prisoners by the law, locked up until faith should be revealed.* ^{24} *So the law was put in charge to lead us to Christ that we might be justified by faith.* ^{25} *Now that faith has come, we are no longer under the supervision of the law.*

The promise was given to Abram. God told Abram that he was going to become a great nation. Abram means "exalted father". His descendants were going to be as numerous as the stars in the sky and as many as the sands on the sea shore. God was calling Abram's descendants to be His people—the mighty nation of Israel. But the promise goes far beyond this. God changes Abram's name to Abraham, which means "father of many". Through Abraham, many nations would be brought into a relationship with God. The promise to Abraham was a blessing to the entire world, even those who were not of Jewish descent. God says, "I will bless the nations through you." The promise came true when Jesus came to earth and died upon the cross. People from all nations were now open to enter into a covenant relationship with God. Jesus is the "Seed" promised to Abraham.

The law came after the promise of the "Seed" God gave Abraham. So how does the law that came later affect the promise? Paul says in verses 17-18, *"What I mean is this: The law, introduced 430 years later, does not set aside the covenant previously established by God and thus do away with the promise. For if the inheritance depends on the law, then it no longer depends on a promise; but God in his grace gave it to Abraham through a promise."* The law does not take away the promised Seed that is to come and bless all nations. Paul goes on to say in verse 19, *"What, then, was the purpose of the law? It was added because of transgressions until the Seed to whom the promise referred had come. The law was put into effect through angels by a mediator."* I hope you see that word "until". The first covenant was based on the law and was put into effect only "until" the Seed came to fulfill the promise to all nations. The little word "until" has a lot of meaning in it. The law was given for us to follow until the Seed came to give us His Spirit to lead us. Romans 10:4 says, *"Christ is the end of the law so that there may be righteousness for everyone who believes."* Christ is the end of the law and the law was put into effect until the Seed comes…because after that, the law is written upon our hearts through the Holy Spirit.

We can also see that in verse 19, "the law was put into effect through angels by a mediator." Hebrews

8:6 says, *"But the ministry Jesus has received is as superior to theirs as the covenant of which he is mediator is superior to the old one, and it is founded on better promises."* God did not use the angels to put the new covenant in effect. It says that God put the promise in effect through His one and only Son, Jesus. Jesus Christ is the mediator of the second and superior covenant.

The old covenant law was intended to be a preliminary to a much greater covenant. The law was there to point us to Christ. Galatians 3:23-25 says, *"Before this faith came, we were held prisoners by the law, locked up until faith should be revealed. So the law was put in charge to lead us to Christ that we might be justified by faith. Now that faith has come, we are no longer under the supervision of the law."* Before the Seed came, we were held as prisoners to the law. We could not get out from under it. We were to follow the law at all times and we could not do it. Again we see the word "until" in verse 23. We were locked up as prisoners to the law "until" faith in Jesus Christ came. Jesus freed us from the law that held us in bondage. What was the purpose of the law then? The law was there to lead us to Christ. The law shows us our need for Him. The following story shows how the law points us to Christ.

> On a warm, summer night, my wife and I were traveling in our car with Micah, our 3-year-old son, who sat in the back seat. After many miles of driving in the darkness, we came to a stop in a remote area. The brightness of the traffic light revealed all of the dirt, dead bugs, and insects on our windshield. Micah said, "Look, how

dirty!" My wife and I didn't think much of his comment until a moment later when we drove on—away from the light and back into the darkness. Upon reentering the darkness, we could no longer see the mess on our windshield, and Micah quickly piped up and said, "Now the glass is clean!" Before the law came, the dirt within us hid under the darkness. But when God gave the law, its light shone on the windshield of our hearts and revealed the filth of sin we'd collected on our journey. The law, then, is a light that shows us how sinful we really are. It cannot cleanse us or make us whole. But it does starkly highlight the true situation of our souls—and thus can lead us to Christ.[7]

Change of law

We see that when Jesus died, there came a change in the way that we interact with God. We do not have to follow the same law that the Israelites had to follow. In the new covenant, Jesus ushers in a new way to view the law. Hebrews 7:11-12 says, *"If perfection could have been attained through the Levitical priesthood (for on the basis of it the law was given to the people), why was there still need for another priest to come—one in the order of Melchizedek, not in the order of Aaron? For when there is a change of the priesthood, there must also be a change of the law."* This verse clearly shows us that we do not have to follow the law that was in effect under the Levitical priest—the priest that was in the order of Aaron. We have a new kind of priesthood, and with a new priesthood is a new law. We now have a priest in the order of Melchizedek. The old covenant law made it perfectly clear that the priests have to come from the tribe of Judah, but Jesus does not trace his lineage back to the Levites. Hebrews 7:14 says, *"For it is clear that our Lord descended from Judah, and in regard to that tribe Moses said nothing about priests."* God would not have allowed a priest to come from the tribe of Judah under the first covenant. So we see the first priesthood under the Levitical law was temporary, like the law it embodied, while the new priesthood will last forever. Hebrews 13:20 says, *"May the God of peace, who through the blood of the eternal covenant brought back from the dead our Lord Jesus, that great Shepherd of the sheep..."* The eternal covenant mentioned in this verse is the new covenant in Jesus' blood. The law is not an eternal covenant that God made with man.

Jesus is now our High Priest. We now follow the law that is written upon our hearts through the Spirit. A good sign of the end of the law is when Jesus was dying on the cross. As Jesus took his last breath, the curtain in the temple was torn completely in two.[8] This was the curtain that separated the Holy Place from the Most Holy Place. In the law, only the High Priest could go in the Most Holy Place, and that was only once a year. Now everyone can enter into the presence of God at anytime because of the blood of Jesus.

The author of Hebrews goes on in chapter 7, verses 18-19, *"The former regulation is set aside because it was weak and useless (for the law made nothing perfect), and a better hope is introduced, by which we draw near to God."* We put aside the old law that was carried out by the old priests, and we now start to live out our lives under our new High Priest. The new covenant is just that—new. It is not a patch of the old covenant.

New Teaching

Jesus introduced a new teaching apart from the law. In Luke 16:16 Jesus says, *"The Law and the Prophets were proclaimed until John. Since that time, the good news of the kingdom of God is being preached, and everyone is forcing his way into it."* "The ministry of John the Baptist, which prepared the way for Jesus the Messiah, was the dividing line between the old covenant and the new."[9] Jesus had a new message apart from the law he wanted to share with the people.

Let's take a closer look at part of Jesus' Sermon on the Mount in Matthew 5. Six times Jesus says, *"You have heard that it was said"*, or something similar to this. Each time Jesus says this, He is referring back to the old covenant law. "The old covenant law says..., but I say ..." Jesus was not standing opposed to the Old Testament law; He was correctly interpreting the true meaning of the law. "The contrast that Jesus sets up is not between the Old Testament and his teachings (he has just established the validity of the Old Testament law). Rather, it is between external interpretations of the rabbinic tradition on the one hand, and Jesus' correct interpretation of the Law on the other."[10] Jesus was teaching the people the true intention of the law—not just what our outward actions should be, but what the internal condition of our hearts should be. It is more about having the character of God than it is about following the outward rituals of the law. Jesus wants us to move beyond the law and to live a life that models His grace. Read the following verses in the Sermon on the Mount where Jesus tells us to go

beyond the written law.
- Matthew 5:21-22 *"You have heard that it was said to the people long ago, 'Do not murder, and anyone who murders will be subject to judgment. But I tell you that anyone who is angry with his brother will be subject to judgment. Again, anyone who says to his brother, 'Raca,' is answerable to the Sanhedrin. But anyone who says, 'You fool!' will be in danger of the fire of hell."*
- Matthew 5:27-28 *"You have heard that it was said, 'Do not commit adultery.' But I tell you that anyone who looks at a woman lustfully has already committed adultery with her in his heart."*
- Matthew 5:31-32 *"It has been said, 'Anyone who divorces his wife must give her a certificate of divorce.' But I tell you that anyone who divorces his wife, except for marital unfaithfulness, causes her to become an adulteress, and anyone who marries the divorced woman commits adultery."*
- Matthew 5:33-35 *"Again, you have heard that it was said to the people long ago, 'Do not break your oath, but keep the oaths you have made to the Lord.' But I tell you, Do not swear at all: either by heaven, for it is God's throne; or by the earth, for it is his footstool; or by Jerusalem, for it is the city of the Great King."*
- Matthew 5:38-40 *"You have heard that it was said, 'Eye for eye, and tooth for tooth.'*

> *But I tell you, Do not resist an evil person. If someone strikes you on the right cheek, turn to him the other also. And if someone wants to sue you and take your tunic, let him have your cloak as well."*
> - Matthew 5:43-44 *"You have heard that it was said, 'Love your neighbor and hate your enemy.' But I tell you: Love your enemies and pray for those who persecute you..."*

Each time in these verses, Jesus says, we need to go beyond what is written in the law. The law was in place to guide us until Jesus came, and now we have a better guide. I came across a good story that I think illustrates the role of the law.

> I often compare the role of the law in history to the role typewriters have played in the development of word processing. The technology and idea of a typewriter was eventually developed into an electronic, faster, and far more complex computer that does word processing. But when typing on a computer, we realize that we are still using the old manual typewriter's technology. Further, we realize that the computer far transcends the typewriter. Everything that a typewriter wanted to be when it was a little boy (and more!) is now found in the computer. This compares to the law. Everything the law wanted

to be when it was young (as revealed to Moses) is found now in Christ and in the life of the Spirit. Thus, when a Christian lives in the Spirit and under Christ, that Christian is not living contrary to the law, but is living in transcendence of the law. It is for this very reason that life lived primarily under the law is wrong. When the computer age arrived, we put away our manual typewriters because they belonged to the former era. Paul's critique of the Judaizers is that they are typing on manual typewriters after computers are on the desk! He calls them to put the manual typewriters away. But in putting them away, we do not destroy them. We fulfill them by typing on the computers. Every maneuver on a computer is the final hope of the manual typewriter. "Now that faith/Christ has come, we are no longer under the supervision of the law"—but not because the law is contrary to the promises; rather, it is because the law is fulfilled in Christ and the Spirit in a manner similar to the way a typewriter is fulfilled in the technology of a computer. And I am profoundly thankful for both![11]

    The law was temporarily in place to point us to a greater reality that is found in Jesus Christ. We are now in a covenant with God through the power of the Spirit.

Chapter 4

Living Under One Covenant

Last chapter we saw that the law had a temporary purpose of bringing us to Christ. The law shows us our need to have a relationship with Jesus Christ in the new covenant that God made with man. Now we must choose which covenant we live under, because we cannot live under two covenants at the same time. Romans chapter 7 helps us understand that we need to die to the first covenant in order to live in the second covenant.

> *¹ Do you not know, brothers—for I am speaking to men who know the law—that the law has authority over a man only as long as he lives? ² For example, by law a married woman is bound to her husband as long as he is alive, but if her husband dies, she is released from the law of marriage. ³ So then, if she marries another man while her husband is still alive, she is called an adulteress. But if her husband dies, she is released from that law and is not an adulteress, even though she marries another man.*
> *⁴ So, my brothers, you also died to*

the law through the body of Christ, that you might belong to another, to him who was raised from the dead, in order that we might bear fruit to God. [5] For when we were controlled by the sinful nature, the sinful passions aroused by the law were at work in our bodies, so that we bore fruit for death. [6] But now, by dying to what once bound us, we have been released from the law so that we serve in the new way of the Spirit, and not in the old way of the written code.

A married woman is bound to her husband for as long as he lives. She cannot marry another, except when he dies, and then she is free to marry again. The Apostle Paul uses this illustration to show our relationship with the two covenants. He shows us that when Christ died, we are freed from the law. Verse 6 says, *"But now, by dying to what once bound us, we have been released from the law so that we serve in the new way of the Spirit, and not in the old way of the written code."* Some people are not free "to marry the Spirit" because they are still holding on to the law. Let me give you an example. If your wife dies, you are free to marry another. You will still think of your deceased wife with fond memories, but you should not cling to her. That would be disrespectful to your new wife. Just like a former deceased spouse, we will continue to remember the old covenant and what it taught, but we should not cling to it.

You cannot be married to both your old husband and the new husband at the same time. You can only be under one covenant. You must choose. In the book of Galatians, that is why Paul is repeatedly mad at them. They continued to hold on to both. They wanted to be married with Christ through the Spirit, but they kept clinging to the law. Paul says in *Galatians 3:1-3, "You foolish Galatians! Who has bewitched you? Before your very eyes Jesus Christ was clearly portrayed as crucified. I would like to learn just one thing from you: Did you receive the Spirit by observing the law, or by believing what you heard? Are you so foolish? After beginning with the Spirit, are you now trying to attain your goal by human effort?"* Paul is making it clear that it is not Christ <u>and</u> the law. It is Christ! Do not disrespect your covenant with Christ because you are still clinging to your old covenant under the law.

    There was a woman who was married to a man who had great expectations upon her. He had a list of things that she was supposed to do every day: Wake up at 5am to make him breakfast, get the kids off to school, do the dishes, clean the house, make him lunch at 12pm, go grocery shopping, do laundry, make him supper at 6pm, help the kids with homework, and the list went on and on. Well, she followed the list that he made for her, but she found no joy in doing the things that he wanted done. Time passed on, and her husband passed away. She ended up getting remarried a few years later. Five years into her new marriage, she found the list that her first husband made for her. She looked over the list, and found that she was doing all the same things for her second husband, but they were not forced upon her. She enjoyed doing these things for her second husband because she was doing it out of the love she had for him.

    This story shows a great picture of the difference of the two covenants. Under the law, the Israelites served

God because it was a list of things they were supposed to do. Now, since we live by the Spirit, we do things for God because we are in a relationship with Jesus and we want to do these things out of love for Him.

Yet there are still people trying to cling to both the law and a relationship with Jesus. Galatians 5:4 says, *"You who are trying to be justified by law have been alienated from Christ; you have fallen away from grace."* If you are still trying to be married to the law, you are alienating yourself from the grace of God. The following is a story explaining that we can only be released from the law when we die.

> It has been said that there is nothing certain but death and taxes. I have never experienced death, but I know something about taxes and I am convinced that the only way to be free from them is to die. Your family might get a bill, but you will be beyond the reach of the IRS. This is what Paul is trying to get us to understand about our new relationship to the Law and to sin. The idea here is that all laws, whether they are God's Laws or man's laws, can only be enforced on a man for as long as he lives. When he dies, he is free from the power of that law. He is beyond its reach. For instance, when Lee Harvey Oswald was arrested for the murder of President John F. Kennedy, he was subject to the laws of the state of Texas and of the United

States of America. However, when Jack Ruby walked into that Dallas police station and killed Oswald, the law could no longer touch him. It would have been foolish of the authorities to have placed him on trial with him being dead! When he died, he was beyond the reach of the law. Spiritually speaking the same is true for the believer. As long as we are alive in our natural state, we are condemned by the Law of God, but when we die, we are free from the demands of the Law. The whole idea of this passage is not to give us a treatise on marriage, but to remind us that the only way to be free from the confines and demands of the Law is for us to be dead. Until we die, the Law hangs over our heads making demands that we can never hope to keep. However, at death, we are set free from these terrible demands.[12]

There is no doubt since we are believers in our Lord Jesus Christ that we are dead. Romans 6:3 says, *"Or don't you know that all of us who were baptized into Christ Jesus were baptized into his death?"* We died along with Christ at our baptism, and we no longer live in the sinful image of the first Adam, but in the life giving Spirit of Jesus.[13] If we are dead, law does not have authority over us.

So what happens to the law? Paul answers that in Romans 3:31. *"Do we, then, nullify the law by this faith? Not at all! Rather, we uphold the law."* "So, has the Law been done away with? No! It is just that we have a different relationship to it than we could ever have had before. Now, because of the imputed righteousness of Jesus and the indwelling ministry of the Holy Spirit, we are able to meet the righteous demands of the Law for the first time. Now, even though we are not under the Law's bondage or its penalties, we want to do what it teaches and we no longer want to live in rebellion against it."[14]

We no longer work tirelessly to try to meet every demand of the law. Instead, we live in a relationship with Jesus, and His Spirit guides us to do the things that please Him. Galatians 3:25 says, *"Now that faith has come, we are no longer under the supervision of the law."* A supervisor is someone who watches over you and makes sure you do what you are supposed to do. They have authority over you. The law is no longer our supervisor. We now get our orders straight from the Spirit of God.

We are no longer under the demands of the law. Paul writes Timothy in 1 Timothy 1:8-11 and says, *"We know that the law is good if one uses it properly. We also know that law is made not for the righteous but for lawbreakers and rebels, the ungodly and sinful, the unholy and irreligious; for those who kill their fathers or mothers, for murderers, for adulterers and perverts, for slave traders and liars and perjurers—and for whatever else is contrary to the sound doctrine that conforms to the glorious gospel of the blessed God, which he entrusted to me."* The law is for people who are not under the new covenant with Jesus. It is clear that the law is not for the righteous. The people in the new covenant are not righteous in themselves, but they are righteous because of what Jesus has done for us. Jesus' righteousness frees us from the demands of the law.

Yoked with Jesus

In Matthew 11: 25-30, *"At that time Jesus said, 'I praise you, Father, Lord of heaven and earth, because you have hidden these things from the wise and learned, and revealed them to little children. Yes, Father, for this was your good pleasure. All things have been committed to me by my Father. No one knows the Son except the Father, and no one knows the Father except the Son and those to whom the Son chooses to reveal him. Come to me, all you who are weary and burdened, and I will give you rest. Take my yoke upon you and learn from me, for I am gentle and humble in heart, and you will find rest for your souls. For my yoke is easy and my burden is light."*

This passage was obviously about the religious leaders of that day, and for the people under the heavy yoke that these religious leaders put on them. Jesus repeatedly speaks against the Pharisees and their self righteousness and putting heavy yokes on the people. Jesus says about the Pharisees in Matthew 23:4, *"They tie up heavy loads and put them on men's shoulders, but they themselves are not willing to lift a finger to move them."* The Pharisees made it impossible for the people to follow the law because of all the rituals they themselves added. So when Jesus said in Matthew 11:25, *"…You have hidden these things from the wise and learned, and revealed them to little children."* He was speaking about the religious leaders who were not following the intention of the law. Immediately after this passage, the religious leaders were judging Jesus' disciples for picking grain on the Sabbath. The Pharisees complained, "That is unlawful to do that on the Sabbath." So it is important to see what is happening in and around this passage—this idea of the religious elite clinging to the laws and Jesus praising the Father for hiding "the gospel" from them.

With this understanding we see in Matthew 11, Jesus uses this idea of a yoke. A yoke is the wooden piece that is placed around the neck of two oxen. This allows the animals to work the field together. You yoke them together. There was a usual way that this would be done—the younger and inexperienced oxen would be yoked next to the mature and stronger oxen. The older oxen would do all of the work and train the younger oxen in what was supposed to be done. The older oxen would carry the load and the younger oxen just needed to keep in step with the older oxen. Can you see the great picture we are given in this passage? Jesus says, *"Take my yoke upon you and learn from me...my burden is light."* Instead of trying to carry the heavy load that the law and the Pharisees put on us, He invites us to take on His yoke. In His yoke, He will do all of the work—all we have to do is keep in step with Jesus. He did the work on the cross—all we have to do is walk with Him. Galatians 5:25 says, *"Since we live by the Spirit, let us keep in step with the Spirit."* We are in this new covenant with the Spirit, and we are to live by His power.

Chapter 5

Accepting Our Inheritance

We now know that Jesus has made it possible for us to inherit the Holy Spirit. If only we would accept this truth. Unfortunately, people are still living as infants in their knowledge of the truth. They haven't received the full promise that is theirs in Christ Jesus. Galatians 4 says,

> *¹ What I am saying is that as long as the heir is a child, he is no different from a slave, although he owns the whole estate. ² He is subject to guardians and trustees until the time set by his father. ³ So also, when we were children, we were in slavery under the basic principles of the world. ⁴ But when the time had fully come, God sent his Son, born of a woman, born under law, ⁵ to redeem those under law, that we might receive the full rights of sons. ⁶ Because you are sons, God sent the Spirit of his Son into our hearts, the Spirit who calls out, "Abba, Father." ⁷ So you are no longer a slave, but a son; and since you are a son, God has made you also an heir.*

Remember in the last chapter how important the word "until" was? We were under the law <u>until</u> faith came. This passage echoes that same thought. A child that is given an inheritance has no access to that inheritance until he comes to be of a certain age. Guardians and trustees are in charge of the inheritance until the child is old enough to receive it. This passage shows that people under the law are children still waiting to receive their inheritance.

We need to remember that the book of Galatians is a letter written by Paul to the Galatian churches. Chapters and verses were added much later in the history of the church as a referencing tool. As you read Galatians, try to read it as a letter. Too often we read Galatians chapter 3 one day, and then the next day we read Galatians 4, then the next day we read Galatians 5, and so on. What we need to see is that this is Paul's continual thought. What he was talking about in chapter 3, continues on uninterrupted into chapter 4, and then into chapter 5. In these three chapters, Paul is laying out the argument that we are not under the law. We saw in Galatians 3:23-25 that, *"Before this faith came, we were held prisoners by the law, locked up until faith should be revealed. So the law was put in charge to lead us to Christ that we might be justified by faith. Now that faith has come, we are no longer under the supervision of the law."* Paul continues on this same point with the passage we just read. As a child we are under the supervision of the law, but when faith appears we receive the full rights as sons. The law cannot touch our inheritance anymore. We have received the inheritance of the Holy Spirit, and we are not subject to the guardians and trustees anymore (law).

Paul was addressing the Galatian churches which would have been made up of both Gentiles and law-following Jews. He was writing to both of them and telling them, "Don't you want to grow up out of your current condition?" Jews are enslaved to the law and Gentiles are enslaved to "the basic principles of the world." Don't you want to grow up and receive the inheritance that can be yours in Christ Jesus? I don't care if you are a Jew or a Gentile, the inheritance of God's Spirit will call you to be a son.

    The Jews were living in bondage and they didn't even realize it. Jesus tried to show them that they were in bondage to the law, but they couldn't see it. They thought that they were free. John 8:31-36 says, *"To the Jews who had believed him, Jesus said, 'If you hold to my teaching, you are really my disciples. Then you will know the truth, and the truth will set you free.' They answered him, 'We are Abraham's descendants and have never been slaves of anyone. How can you say that we shall be set free?' Jesus replied, 'I tell you the truth, everyone who sins is a slave to sin. Now a slave has no permanent place in the family, but a son belongs to it forever. So if the Son sets you free, you will be free indeed.'"* The Pharisees in this passage couldn't see their bondage to the law. Jesus came to set them free from the law and to make them "a son" forever. Instead, they choose to stay a slave to the law. Paul is echoing Jesus' thoughts in Galatians and uses strong language towards the churches. *"You foolish Galatians!"*[15] They were trying to mix the saving power of Jesus' work on the cross with the law. They were trying to mix the new covenant with the old covenant. Many people in today's churches are doing the same thing. They are still bound like the Pharisees and they don't realize it. Read Jesus' words in John 8:36, *"So if the Son sets you free, you will be free indeed."* You are not half-way free. Jesus has power to free us from the law, because He completely fulfilled it on our behalf. Paul says in the next chapter of Galatians, Galatians 5:1, *"It is for freedom that Christ has set us free. Stand firm, then, and do not let yourselves be burdened again by a yoke of slavery."* What kind of slavery was Paul talking about here? It is what he has been speaking of throughout Galatians. They were burdened, or in slavery, by trying to follow all the regulations of the law. As we saw in chapter four, we are to be in a yoke with Jesus in the new covenant which brings us freedom from the law.

Verse 4 tells us that this Son was "born under the law." "Jesus submitted to all the law. He was circumcised the eighth day; His parents provided all the proper sacrifices for him. He fulfilled all the law. He did this to 'redeem them that are under the law.' Christ satisfies all the law. He met its every demand. The law can demand no longer! To summarize Paul's argument, Jewish law (any law system) is for children who are not yet recognized as sons."[16]

Paul tells us that when the time came, God sent Jesus into the world to give us full rights as sons. John 1:12 says, *"Yet to all who received him, to those who believed in his name, he gave the right to become children of God."* It was not the people who continued to live descent lives under the law that God gave this great privilege to. It was the people who believed in Him and received God's wondrous grace. This Galatians 4 passage says that we get this right to become sons when we come of age. Paul is not referring to a certain age limit and saying that we will automatically become Sons of God. It is not like the Jewish culture, where at the age of 13 they have a Bar Mitzvah to be considered part of the family of God. Or today people could say, "Well, most of the people at my church get baptized as a freshman in high school. So I will get baptized and become part of the family of God." No, we become an adopted son or daughter of God, only when we have died to ourselves and started living for him. There is no magical age that we receive the inheritance of God's Spirit. However, there is an inheritance when "we grow up in the faith".

If we jump ahead in Galatians 4, we read,

> *21 Tell me, you who want to be under the law, are you not aware of what the law says? 22 For it is written that Abraham had two sons, one by the slave woman and the other by the free woman. 23 His son by the slave woman was born in the ordinary way; but his son by the free woman was born as the result of a promise.*
>
> *24 These things may be taken figuratively, for the women represent two covenants. One covenant is from Mount Sinai and bears children who are to be slaves: This is Hagar. 25 Now Hagar stands for Mount Sinai in Arabia and corresponds to the present city of Jerusalem, because she is in slavery with her children. 26 But the Jerusalem that is above is free, and she is our mother. 27 For it is written:*
>
>> *"Be glad, O barren woman,*
>> *who bears no children;*

> *break forth and cry aloud,*
> *you who have no labor pains;*
> *because more are the children of the desolate woman than of her who has a husband."*
> ²⁸ Now you, brothers, like Isaac, are children of promise. ²⁹ At that time the son born in the ordinary way persecuted the son born by the power of the Spirit. It is the same now. ³⁰ But what does the Scripture say? "Get rid of the slave woman and her son, for the slave woman's son will never share in the inheritance with the free woman's son." ³¹ Therefore, brothers, we are not children of the slave woman, but of the free woman.

In this passage, Paul is giving us a choice between two covenants. One is obedience to the law, and the other covenant is based on the promise of God. Paul is discouraged because he sees the Galatian churches choosing to follow the wrong covenant. Because of this, he starts off this passage by saying, "Are you sure you want to be under the law? Don't you know what the law says?" Then he uses the example of the two sons of Abraham. He correlates the two sons of Abraham with what we know as the new and old covenants. Hagar's son, Ishmael, was born to Abraham in the ordinary way. Hagar was a slave and Paul says that her son represented the covenant that God made with Israel at Mt. Sinai. It was at Sinai that the Ten Commandments were given to

Moses. Most people believe that the book of Galatians is talking about circumcision when it says that we are not under the law, but circumcision was not given to Moses at Sinai. It was given to Abraham many generations earlier. Paul is talking about becoming a slave to the law.

Abraham and Sarah were promised by God that they would have a son. Unfortunately, they didn't wait for the child God promised them, but instead they tried with their own reasoning to have a child. Sarah told Abraham to marry her maidservant so that they could have a child through her. Paul shows us that this child represents the covenant that relied on works, not on God's power. This son was born in a way that is completely different than the second son of Abraham.

The second child, Isaac, was born through a promise. He was born of a free woman who was well past her childbearing years. Abraham was 99 and Sarah was 89 years old. God was waiting until they were both "as good as dead".[17] He wanted to show them beyond a shadow of a doubt that this child was from Him. This child could not have been born apart from God's intervention. Isaac represents the freedom that we have in the new covenant. The new covenant has nothing to do with our works, but has everything to do with God intervening on our behalf.

Paul sums up this passage in verses 30-31, *"But what does the Scripture say? 'Get rid of the slave woman and her son, for the slave woman's son will never share in the inheritance with the free woman's son.' Therefore, brothers, we are not children of the slave woman, but of the free woman."* We are to get rid of the slave woman and her son. It is clear that Paul was telling the Galatians to free themselves from the law. The slave woman's son will not share in the inheritance with the free woman's son. Those under the law will not receive the promise of God. You can't receive the promise of God through the law! It is impossible. We are children of the free woman, and therefore, we will inherit the power of the Spirit.

Let's look below at the differences Paul points out between the two covenants in this passage.[18]

Two Mothers- Hagar and Sarah
Two Sons- Ishmael and Isaac
Two Covenants- Works and Grace
Two Cities- Earthly Jerusalem and Jerusalem above
Two Mountains- Sinai and Calvary
Flesh and Promise- Law and Faith
Slavery and Children- Bondage and Freedom
Natural and Spiritual- Attainment and Grace

"Now the purpose of this allegory, as Paul uses it, is to show us the believer's complete and total freedom from the law. No two things in the entire world are more diametrically opposed to one another than law and grace, which is nothing more or less than the heretical assertion that salvation is by our works and the gospel declaration that we are saved by God's free grace through the obedience and death of the Lord Jesus Christ. We must understand the difference between these two things. Any mixture of law and grace, any intermingling of the covenant of works with the covenant of grace is deadly."[19] Don't be children under the law, but grow up in your salvation through the faith that is found in Jesus Christ.

Chapter 6

The New Commandments

In the first five chapters we have seen that we are not under the law. So now what? How are we supposed to live? If we are not under the law, what are the guidelines that we need to live under in the new covenant? In Matthew chapter 22, Jesus gives us some new commandments that we need to live by in the new covenant.

> [34] Hearing that Jesus had silenced the Sadducees, the Pharisees got together. [35] One of them, an expert in the law, tested him with this question: [36] "Teacher, which is the greatest commandment in the Law?"
> [37] Jesus replied: "'Love the Lord your God with all your heart and with all your soul and with all your mind.' [38] This is the first and greatest commandment. [39] And the second is like it: 'Love your neighbor as yourself.' [40] All the Law and the Prophets hang on these two commandments."

Jesus was publicly teaching the people and the

religious leaders who were trying to stump him with hard questions regarding the law. The Sadducees and Pharisees had several differences in their beliefs but they both made up the Sanhedrin which was the religious ruling council.[20] They came together for the common goal of catching Jesus in His words about the law in front of the people. Right before this passage, the Sadducees had just finished asking Jesus about one part of the law, and Jesus said in verse 29, *"You are in error because you do not know the Scriptures or the power of God."* So now it was the Pharisees' turn to try to trap Jesus in some aspect of the law. So one of them asked, *"Teacher, which is the greatest commandment in the Law?"* The religious leaders had a hierarchy of which laws were more serious. "Jewish rabbis counted 613 individual statutes in the law, and attempted to differentiate between 'heavy' (or 'great') and 'light' (or 'little') commands."[21] This man wanted to know from Jesus, which ones are the heavy ones that I need to follow. I imagine them expecting Jesus to quote some of the Ten Commandments.

    Many people today put a lot of focus on the Ten Commandments and how important they think they are, but when Jesus was asked, "What is the greatest commandment?" He did not quote any of the Ten Commandments. Instead, He quoted Deuteronomy 6:5 and Leviticus 19:18. Deuteronomy 6:5 says, *"Love the LORD your God with all your heart and with all your soul and with all your strength."* And Leviticus 19:18 says, *"Do not seek revenge or bear a grudge against one of your people, but love your neighbor as yourself. I am the LORD."* This would have been a great time for Jesus to tell the man, "All of the Ten Commandments are important—there are no unimportant commandments." Jesus doesn't even hint that any one of the Ten

Commandments is more important than "Love God and Love your Neighbor." In fact, Mark 12 shares the same story found here in Matthew 22, but Mark finishes with Jesus saying in verse 31, *"...There is no commandment greater than these."* Jesus gave us the heart and the soul of the law in these two commandments. If you follow the two commandments that Jesus gives here, you will completely follow the Ten Commandments and the rest of the law perfectly.

Love is the fulfillment of the law. Verse 40 says, *"All the Law and the Prophets hang on these two commandments."* Would you see a need for the law if people really did live out the two greatest commandments that Jesus gives in these verses? If we loved God and loved people, everything else would fall into place. We wouldn't have to worry about someone murdering, because they love. No one would commit adultery because of love, and people wouldn't want to hurt others intentionally. Love is the fulfillment of the law. Romans 13:8-10 says, *"Let no debt remain outstanding, except the continuing debt to love one another, for he who loves his fellowman has fulfilled the law. The commandments, 'Do not commit adultery,' 'Do not murder,' 'Do not steal,' 'Do not covet,' and whatever other commandments there may be, are summed up in this one rule: 'Love your neighbor as yourself.' Love does no harm to its neighbor. Therefore love is the fulfillment of the law."* Twice in these three verses Paul says that love is the fulfillment of the law. Paul also tells the Galatian churches in Galatians 5:14, *"The entire law is summed up in a single command: 'Love your neighbor as yourself.'"* Why do Christian churches today reference the Ten Commandments more than we do the two greatest commandments we get from Jesus? If we live out the "Two Commandments" in the new covenant we will fulfill the entire law!

James also refers to these words of Jesus. James says in James 2:8, *"If you really keep the royal law found in Scripture, 'Love your neighbor as yourself,' you are doing right."* James calls "love your neighbor" the royal law. "The law is royal or regal (*basilikon,* from *basileus,* "king") because it was decreed by the King of kings."[22] Jesus simplifies the law for us in two quick sentences. "Love God. Love people." Follow these instructions and you will live a completely pleasing life before God.

In John chapter 13, Jesus is telling His disciples that His death is coming up quickly. It was actually this very night that Jesus was going to be arrested. This was the last evening that He was going to be with His disciples before He would die upon the cross. You can expect that Jesus was going to get one last message across to them that they really needed to hear. This was no time for small talk. Verses 33-35 Jesus says, *"My children, I will be with you only a little longer. You will look for me, and just as I told the Jews, so I tell you now: Where I am going, you cannot come. A new command I give you: Love one another. As I have loved you, so you must love one another. By this all men will know that you are my disciples, if you love one another."* Jesus did not talk about tithing, lying, gossiping or even adultery. The last message He had for His disciples was about love. Jesus gives them one last command before He goes to the cross. *"As I have loved you, so you must love one another."* Why didn't Jesus talk about some aspect of the law that the disciples really needed to know? Because we see that Jesus wanted to give them a new commandment, *"Love one another."*

How can Jesus say that this is a "new" command?

Love others was something that people were to be doing throughout the Old Testament. When you look at the context of this verse, Jesus just finished eating the Lord's Supper with His disciples. We call it the Lord's Supper because that is where Jesus broke the bread and passed around the wine saying it was His body and blood. Jesus was instituting the new covenant with His disciples in the room. He would later officially bring about the new covenant by dying on the cross. But just as Jesus institutes the new covenant, He gives them the commandment to live in this new covenant. *"A new command I give you: Love one another. As I have loved you, so you must love one another."*

People knew that you were in the old covenant if you were circumcised and if you lived your life in obedience to the law. Jesus says, "People will know you are living in the new covenant if you love one another."(Kurt Litwiller Version) That is what Jesus is saying in verse 35, *"By this, people will know you are my disciples, if you love one another."*

Chapter 7

Approaching God

The old covenant and the new covenant have many differences, but none of those differences are as drastic as how you can approach God. The law does not give you access into God's presence like the blood of Jesus does. This chapter alone makes it worthwhile to live in the new covenant relationship with God. Let's look at Hebrews 12 and see what it says about the difference in approaching God when considering the two covenants.

> *18 You have not come to a mountain that can be touched and that is burning with fire; to darkness, gloom and storm; 19 to a trumpet blast or to such a voice speaking words that those who heard it begged that no further word be spoken to them, 20 because they could not bear what was commanded: "If even an animal touches the mountain, it must be stoned." 21 The sight was so terrifying that Moses said, "I am trembling with fear."*
> *22 But you have come to Mount Zion, to the heavenly Jerusalem, the city*

> *of the living God. You have come to thousands upon thousands of angels in joyful assembly, ²³ to the church of the firstborn, whose names are written in heaven. You have come to God, the judge of all men, to the spirits of righteous men made perfect, ²⁴ to Jesus the mediator of a new covenant, and to the sprinkled blood that speaks a better word than the blood of Abel.*

In this passage we have two mountains, each of which stands for a different covenant that God made with man. The first mountain, Mount Sinai, represents the old covenant in which God gave the Ten Commandments to Moses so that he could share them with the people. The second mountain, Mount Zion, stands for the heavenly kingdom that we have through Jesus Christ in the new covenant. This passage obviously gives us differences in how we can approach God in these two covenants.

Approaching God in the Old Covenant

The author of Hebrews starts with how the people of Israel approached God while they were under the law of the old covenant. He refers us back to the story in Exodus 19, when God was going to give the people the Ten Commandments. God says in Exodus 19:12-13, *"Put limits for the people around the mountain and tell them, 'Be careful that you do not go up the mountain or touch the foot of it. Whoever touches the mountain shall surely be put to death. He shall surely be stoned or shot with arrows; not a hand is to be laid on him. Whether man or animal, he shall not be permitted to live.' Only when the ram's horn sounds a long blast may they go up to the mountain."* In the old covenant the people couldn't even touch the mountain that God's presence was upon.

We see this same thought throughout the entire old covenant. The people could not have access to God. God's Spirit dwelled in the temple in the Most Holy Place, and common man could not enter God's presence. Hebrews 9:7 tells us, *"But only the high priest entered the inner room, and that only once a year, and never without blood, which he offered for himself and for the sins the people had committed in ignorance."* In the old covenant we could not approach God because we were still blemished by sin. We know that at the beginning of creation man had unbroken fellowship with God. They enjoyed the very presence of God. However, once sin entered the world, God could no longer dwell with man. God is Holy and He cannot associate with sin. So we see, even in the old covenant relationship with God, we could not enter His presence because we still remained corrupted in our sin. Hebrews 10:1-4 says, *"The law is only a shadow of the good things that are coming—not the realities themselves. For this reason it can never, by the same sacrifices repeated endlessly year after year, make perfect those who draw near to worship. If it could, would they not have stopped being offered? For the worshipers would have been cleansed once for all, and would no longer have felt guilty for their sins. But those sacrifices are an annual reminder of sins, because it is impossible for the blood of bulls and goats to take away sins."* Did you hear that last verse? *"...it is impossible for the blood of bulls and goats to take away sins."* Later in Hebrews 10, it says in verse 11, *"Day after day every priest stands and performs his religious duties; again and again he offers the same sacrifices, which can never take away sins."* I feel like I could go on and quote all of Hebrews chapters 7-10 to you. Instead, I challenge you to read these four chapters for yourself.

The point being, the old covenant could not take away sins! So people could not approach God in the old covenant. They needed a mediator, and that mediator was a high priest who also had sins in his life. He offered the sacrifice for himself, as well as for the people, once a year. The mediator of the old covenant was not perfect, nor did he bring a perfect sacrifice to God.

God's presence dwelled in the Ark of the Covenant (which we will look at in detail in chapter 9), and so the Israelites could not come close to the ark. Only the priests could carry the ark, in which they were to only touch the poles—they themselves couldn't even touch the ark. One time the ark was being moved from one place to another and someone touched it. We see in 2 Samuel 6: 6-7 what happened. *"When they came to the threshing floor of Nacon, Uzzah reached out and took hold of the ark of God, because the oxen stumbled. The LORD's anger burned against Uzzah because of his irreverent act; therefore God struck him down and he died there beside the ark of God."* No one could touch the ark because it represented God's presence. Only the priests could be close to it since they were God's chosen people to work with the tabernacle. When Israel was in the wilderness and they were transporting the ark from one campsite to another, there were rules about what the Israelites should do to the ark. In Joshua 3:3-4 we see the instructions the people were given about how close they could come to the ark, *"...giving orders to the people: 'When you see the ark of the covenant of the LORD your God, and the priests, who are Levites, carrying it, you are to move out from your positions and follow it. Then you will know which way to go, since you have never been this way before. But keep a distance of about a thousand yards between you and the ark; do not go near it.'"* Under the old covenant relationship, the people were not allowed to go near the ark because that was the very presence of God.

Approaching God in the New Covenant

Hebrews 12:18 says, *"You have not come to a mountain that can be touched",* and verse 22 picks up this point and says, *"But you have come to Mount Zion, to the heavenly Jerusalem, the city of the living God."* The author of Hebrews talks in great length about how we are not under the law. The mountain in verse 18 is a physical mountain that can be touched, though it would bring death if the Israelites did touch it. Where as we come to Mount Zion, the heavenly city of God, which cannot be physically touched. We do so in faith because we cannot see heaven with our physical eyes.

We see a turning point on how we can approach God, when Jesus was dying upon the cross. Matthew 27:51 says, *"At that moment the curtain of the temple was torn in two from top to bottom. The earth shook and the rocks split."* I mentioned this in chapter 3, but the curtain that was torn was the curtain between the Holy Place and the Most Holy Place. God's Presence dwelled in the Most Holy Place. The high priest was the only one that could go into the Most Holy Place and that was only once a year. Jesus dying on the cross ushered in the new covenant, and by His blood we are forgiven. The curtain, being torn in two, was a sign that we can all enter into God's presence, not just the high priest.

The High Priest in the second covenant, Jesus, was perfect. He had no sin. He also brought the perfect sacrifice—Himself. Hebrews 9:12 says, *"He did not enter by means of the blood of goats and calves; but he entered the Most Holy Place once for all by his own blood, having obtained eternal redemption."* His blood was not a temporary fix to our sin problem like the old covenant sacrifices. His blood was shed <u>once</u> for our eternal redemption. He covered our past, present, and future sins as long as we remain in the new covenant relationship with Him.

The attitude with which we approach God in the new covenant is completely different as well. In the old covenant, the people approached God with trembling. They saw the smoke on the mountain and they trembled. They knew that they could not be in God's presence. Just like Adam and Eve after they sinned, they hid from God. They knew that they could not be in God's presence because of their sin and shame. While in the new covenant, we can approach God with confidence. Hebrews 10:19-20 says, *"Therefore, brothers, since we have confidence to enter the Most Holy Place by the blood of Jesus, by a new and living way opened for us through the curtain, that is, his body."* Hebrews 4:16 also says, *"Let us then approach the throne of grace with confidence, so that we may receive mercy and find grace to help us in our time of need."* We know that Jesus' perfect sacrifice has taken away our sins once and for all, so we can approach Him with confidence. What a difference there is in approaching God's Presence when contrasting the two covenants. In the old covenant you would be killed, but in the new covenant we can come into His Presence with confidence.

Verse 24 says, *"...to Jesus the mediator of a new*

covenant, and to the sprinkled blood that speaks a better word than the blood of Abel." Abel was the first person to be murdered in the Bible. His blood cries out for vengeance. The law was given to man after sin entered the world and then there needed to be some guidelines for men to live under. The new covenant of Jesus restores us back to more of the ways in the garden. We are in a relationship with God, not under laws that we need to follow. Jesus' blood does not cry out for vengeance, but for restoration.

"These verses describe the awesome occasion when the law was given at Mount Sinai, a description focusing on the old covenant's tangible mountain, ordinances, terrifying warnings and severe penalties. Believers in Jesus Christ do not have such a threatening covenant, and should not consider returning to it."[23] There were many in early Christendom that were convinced to go back to practice the law along with their faith in Jesus Christ. This passage clearly shows us that the two covenants are very separate in what they have to offer. The author of Hebrews is warning the people not to go back to the law, but to live with confidence in the new covenant. My fellow Christians, don't go back to a way of life that was never meant for you.

Chapter 8

A Covenant Symbol

There is always a symbol to show that you are entering into a covenant relationship with someone (an agreement between two parties). For instance, when you enter into the covenant relationship of marriage, rings are exchanged to show that you accept the vows that you make to one another. You promise to live out your vows. It is the same way in our relationship with God. The old covenant had a symbol to show that the Israelites were in a covenant relationship with God, just as the new covenant has a different symbol to acknowledge those who enter into this new agreement. Let's first look at the covenant symbol of the old covenant. In Genesis 17 it says,

> [9] *Then God said to Abraham, "As for you, you must keep my covenant, you and your descendants after you for the generations to come.* [10] *This is my covenant with you and your descendants after you, the covenant you are to keep: Every male among you shall be circumcised.* [11] *You are to undergo circumcision, and it will be the sign of the covenant between me and you.* [12] *For the generations to come every male among you who is*

eight days old must be circumcised, including those born in your household or bought with money from a foreigner—those who are not your offspring. ¹³ Whether born in your household or bought with your money, they must be circumcised. My covenant in your flesh is to be an everlasting covenant. ¹⁴ Any uncircumcised male, who has not been circumcised in the flesh, will be cut off from his people; he has broken my covenant."

Verse 14 gives us an understanding of how important circumcision was to the Israelites. *"Any uncircumcised male, who has not been circumcised in the flesh, will be cut off from his people; he has broken my covenant."* No one wanted to be cut off from God's promises. Being circumcised was the price people were willing to pay to be a part of God's people, even when they forgot why they were circumcised in the first place. Circumcision was supposed to be an act of obedience and submission, but the Israelites turned it into something that they did as a ritual. Circumcision was supposed to be a statement that "I live only for you, God", but it became more of a symbol, like belonging a country club.

Picture someone telling you that if you were to take off your wedding ring, your covenant relationship with your spouse would be over. Your ring is the everlasting sign that you are married to your spouse. We know that we are not married because of a ring that we wear on our finger. The ring is just the outward sign of the commitment that we made. I can be married to my wife whether I wear a ring or not. There are many people who wear the wedding ring, but are not in the covenant relationship with their spouse. They sneak around and cheat on their spouse and offer them no respect. But that must be alright, because they have their wedding ring on, so that proves they are in a covenant relationship with their spouse, right? No! A symbol doesn't necessarily mean that you are living according to the vows of the covenant. I wonder if this is how God felt with the people in the old covenant relationship. People became circumcised and then went out and did things that were against the covenant agreement. The people could say, "Hey, I am still in this covenant relationship with God. See, I was circumcised." God doesn't care so much about our outward allegiance. He cares about being in a relationship with us.

Circumcision was a sign that the Israelites were God's people. In verse 13 of Genesis chapter 17, God says, *"...My covenant in your flesh is to be an everlasting covenant."* This was to be an everlasting covenant with God, but we see that Paul preaches against circumcision in the New Testament. How can that be if circumcision is supposed to be an everlasting sign? Romans 2:28-29 Paul says, *"A man is not a Jew if he is only one outwardly, nor is circumcision merely outward and physical. No, a man is a Jew if he is one inwardly; and circumcision is circumcision of the heart, by the Spirit, not by the written code. Such a man's praise is not from men, but from God."* The circumcision was everlasting, but it needs to be a circumcision of the heart. They mistook this outward act, as the only thing that needed to be done. This outward act was only a symbol of what should be happening inwardly. God is more concerned about the heart than He is about our flesh. Many people today treat the law in the same way that the Old Testament people treated circumcision. "It is an everlasting covenant with God. We can't do away with it." An important thing we need to see is this—just as circumcision went from an outward act to an inward act, so the law went from the written word, to being written on our hearts through the Spirit of God. Circumcision is still followed today, but it is a circumcision of the heart. The law is still followed today, but instead it is followed through obedience to the Holy Spirit.

The Apostles reject old covenant symbol

Knowing that circumcision was the sign of entering into the old covenant, we see in the New Testament that people tried to force circumcision on believers of Jesus Christ. They wanted people to live out both the new and old covenants.

Paul and Barnabas had been out spreading the gospel of Jesus Christ, and they came upon some Jewish believers who were insistent on Gentiles being circumcised. In Acts 15:1, people were saying, *"...Unless you are circumcised, according to the custom taught by Moses, you cannot be saved."* Paul and Barnabas did not believe that was the case, so they went up to Jerusalem to see what the Apostles had to say. Let's continue on in Acts 15 as the Apostles in Jerusalem tackle this tough subject.

> *5 Then some of the believers who belonged to the party of the Pharisees stood up and said, "The Gentiles must be circumcised and required to obey the law of Moses."*

> *⁶ The apostles and elders met to consider this question. ⁷ After much discussion, Peter got up and addressed them: "Brothers, you know that some time ago God made a choice among you that the Gentiles might hear from my lips the message of the gospel and believe. ⁸ God, who knows the heart, showed that he accepted them by giving the Holy Spirit to them, just as he did to us. ⁹ He made no distinction between us and them, for he purified their hearts by faith. ¹⁰ Now then, why do you try to test God by putting on the necks of the disciples a yoke that neither we nor our fathers have been able to bear? ¹¹ No! We believe it is through the grace of our Lord Jesus that we are saved, just as they are."*

The Pharisees, the "guardians" of the law, said that people needed to be circumcised. There were some Pharisees who did believe in Jesus, but they wanted to continue in their Judaic beliefs as well. There were many in the time of the New Testament that thought people had to be converted to Judaism before they could become Christians. They thought, "We have to live under the first covenant before we can receive the second covenant. We need to live under the law to receive the Spirit."

As we read these verses, we could think that this is only about circumcision, but it goes well beyond that. This is about keeping the entire law that is found in the old covenant. We know that because Peter says in verse 10, *"Now then, why do you try to test God by putting on the necks of the disciples a yoke that neither we nor our fathers have been able to bear?"* It is clear that Peter is talking about more than just circumcision. If the discussion is only about circumcision, circumcision is a yoke that people could actually bare. It is only one painful surgery which welcomes a man into the group of believers. But the phrase, *"a yoke that neither we nor our fathers have been able to bear"*, is referencing the whole law. No one can keep the whole law. So Peter goes on to say in verse 11, *"No! We believe it is through the grace of our Lord Jesus that we are saved, just as they are."* Peter boldly declares, "They are saved the same way we are. We are not saved because we are circumcised. We are saved because of the grace we have received through Jesus." The early church took a strong stand against the culture of that day and said, "It is not the law that saves. You are not under law. The Gentiles do not need to be circumcised according to the law."

This would not have been an easy stand for the church to take because it was not a decision that made sense to the people. Peter even caved under the peer pressure of those who lived under the law. Paul had to confront Peter in Galatians 2. Verses 11-14 say, *"When Peter came to Antioch, I opposed him to his face, because he was clearly in the wrong. Before certain men came from James, he used to eat with the Gentiles. But when they arrived, he began to draw back and separate himself from the Gentiles because he was afraid of those who belonged to the circumcision group. The other Jews joined him in his hypocrisy, so that by their hypocrisy even Barnabas was led astray. When I saw that they were not acting in line with the truth of the gospel, I said* to Peter in front of them all, "You are a Jew, yet you live like a Gentile and not like a Jew. How is it, then, that you force Gentiles to follow Jewish customs?" Peter was obviously a little nervous at times to stand up for the freedom that he had from the law. He gladly over looked the law and ate with Gentiles while he was with a certain group of people, but when the Jewish elite from Jerusalem came, he started to act like a "true Jew." Paul accuses Peter of living like a Gentile, while making the Gentiles follow Jewish customs. Paul wanted to make sure he didn't lose any ground in his fight against the incorrect doctrine of the Jews.

In Acts 15:21 the Apostles say, *"For Moses has been preached in every city from the earliest times and is read in the synagogues on every Sabbath."* Don't misinterpret this verse. They are not saying that the Law of Moses is still in effect, but that it was the only Word of God that they had at that time to study. The gospels had not yet been written, Paul had not written his epistles, Peter had not written his letters, and John had not written his books of the Bible yet. All they had to study was the Law of Moses and how Jesus came to fulfill those laws. Acts 17: 1-3 talks about how Paul used the scriptures (or Law of Moses), *"When they had passed through Amphipolis and Apollonia, they came to Thessalonica, where there was a Jewish synagogue. As his custom was, Paul went into the synagogue, and on three Sabbath days he reasoned with them from the Scriptures, explaining and proving that the Christ had to suffer and rise from the dead. 'This Jesus I am proclaiming to you is the Christ,' he said."* The early church used the Law of Moses (Old Testament scriptures) to convince the people that Jesus came to bring them new life.

If you have read the New Testament, you know

that circumcision was a big deal to the Jewish people. Paul repeatedly teaches that the church does not need to be circumcised. Paul was adamant in his fight against circumcision. He made a line in the sand and said that this was the teaching that everything else is built upon. This foundation must be agreed upon by all Christians because circumcision was the sign that you are entering the old covenant.

Circumcision put you on the wrong path to God. You would still be following God through the law of the Old Testament. However, circumcision was a tough practice for the Jewish people to let go of because it showed that they were accepted and in a covenant relationship with God through the law that God gave them. The early church leaders were faithful and stood against persecution to preserve the truth found in Jesus Christ—that it is not by observing the law that you are saved, but it is by grace in Jesus Christ. It was a big step for the Apostles to declare, "Circumcision is no longer needed. We are no longer accepting applications for the old covenant. There is something far better. Everyone moves directly into the new covenant."

The New Covenant Symbol

The Apostles abandoned the old covenant symbol of circumcision and started to teach the new covenant symbol of baptism. After Jesus' ascension to heaven, people were convicted of their sins and they asked Peter, "What should we do?" Acts 2:38 says, *"Peter replied, 'Repent and be baptized, every one of you, in the name of Jesus Christ for the forgiveness of your sins. And you will receive the gift of the Holy Spirit.'"* Peter's first question to the people was not, "Have you all been circumcised? That would be the first step if you haven't been." No,

Peter tells them to repent of their sins and then enter into the new covenant with God through baptism. After baptism, they would not receive a book of all of the laws that they needed to follow. He told them that they would receive the Holy Spirit, who would give them the power to live a faithful life before God. The law could not do that!

If you look at the symbolism in baptism, you can clearly see that baptism is a great picture of the new covenant agreement that we have with God. Romans 6: 4-5 says, *"We were therefore buried with him through baptism into death in order that, just as Christ was raised from the dead through the glory of the Father, we too may live a new life. If we have been united with him like this in his death, we will certainly also be united with him in his resurrection."* When we are baptized we are dying to ourselves. The word for baptism in the original Greek language means to "immerse". As we are baptized we are completely immersed in the water—we are being buried to symbolize that we are united with Christ in His death. Then we are brought up out of the water to indicate the new life we have received in Christ Jesus. We died to our sinful nature and we are raised to a new powerful life in the Spirit.

We need to be careful that we don't make baptism just a ritual like the Jews did with circumcision. We need to understand that baptism is our way of showing our allegiance to God. We still have to walk the talk after we are baptized. We vow to him at baptism to follow him all the days of our lives. Baptism in itself cannot save anyone. It is only an outward sign of what the Spirit of God is doing to us inwardly. Just going through a baptism ceremony doesn't make you a Christian, just like being circumcised makes you a Jew.[24] These are outward symbols to show that you are committing yourself to a relationship with God.

If you read on a little further in Romans 6, you come to verse 14, *"For sin shall not be your master, because you are not under law, but under grace."* There again is that one covenant living idea. If you are under the new covenant through baptism, you are not under law. You are under the power of the Spirit that directs you in the true intention of the law.

The covenant symbols of both the old and new covenants point to the fact that we are not under law. The law was put aside so that we can serve God inwardly from the heart, not by the letter of the law.

Chapter 9

Judged By Law?

Maybe there are some of you out there who are still convinced that we are under the law. You may be thinking, "If we are not under the law, how are we going to be judged?" I saved this heavy, in-depth study for one of the last chapters. This chapter will really get you excited about digging into the Word of God. I know that I was in awe as I was writing this chapter. In Exodus 25, God gives Moses the instructions on how to overlay the Ark of the Covenant.

> [17] *"Make an atonement cover of pure gold—two and a half cubits long and a cubit and a half wide.* [18] *And make two cherubim out of hammered gold at the ends of the cover.* [19] *Make one cherub on one end and the second cherub on the other; make the cherubim of one piece with the cover, at the two ends.* [20] *The cherubim are to have their wings spread upward, overshadowing the cover with them. The cherubim are to face each other, looking toward the cover.* [21] *Place the cover on top of the ark and put in the ark the Testimony, which I will give you.* [22] *There, above the cover*

between the two cherubim that are over the ark of the Testimony, I will meet with you and give you all my commands for the Israelites.

God was clear on how Moses was supposed to lay out the tabernacle and how he was supposed to cover the Ark of the Covenant. Why is this endeavor such a big deal? Hebrews 8:5 says, *"They serve at a sanctuary that is a copy and shadow of what is in heaven. This is why Moses was warned when he was about to build the tabernacle: 'See to it that you make everything according to the pattern shown you on the mountain.'"* When Moses was on the mountain, God gave him specific instructions on what the sanctuary and the things in it should look like. The reason was because it was a copy of the perfect tabernacle which is in heaven.

The Ark of the Covenant was put in the Most Holy Place—no one could enter that room but the high priest once a year. God's presence was in the Most Holy Place. God was so specific on how to build the ark, because the ark was the copy of His throne in heaven. The ark was supposed to have two cherubim that covered the ark. There are many places in scripture that say the same thing as Isaiah 37:16, *"O LORD Almighty, God of Israel, enthroned between the cherubim, you alone are God over all the kingdoms of the earth. You have made heaven and earth."*[25] The Lord dwells between the cherubim. We see throughout scripture that God's throne is between the two cherubim. One day Moses went into the tabernacle to speak with the Lord, and it says in Numbers 7:89, *"When Moses entered the Tent of Meeting to speak with the LORD, he heard the voice speaking to him from* between the two cherubim above the atonement cover on the ark of the Testimony. And he spoke with him." The ark was the copy of God's throne in heaven. It was not the acacia wood, the cherubim, or the gold that made the ark sacred, but it was God's presence. His presence was on His earthly throne to lead Israel.

1 Kings 8:9 tells us what was in the Ark of the Covenant. *"There was nothing in the ark except the two stone tablets that Moses had placed in it at Horeb, where the LORD made a covenant with the Israelites after they came out of Egypt."*[26] Some people may think that there was possibly more than just the Ten Commandments in the Ark of the Covenant. They believe that because of what it says in Hebrews 9:3-4. *"Behind the second curtain was a room called the Most Holy Place, which had the golden altar of incense and the gold-covered ark of the covenant. This ark contained the gold jar of manna, Aaron's staff that had budded, and the stone tablets of the covenant."* The author of Hebrews says that the gold jar of manna and Aaron's budding staff were also in the ark of the covenant along with the Ten Commandments. But we know that is not true from other verses that we see in the Old Testament. Exodus 16:33-34 says, *"So Moses said to Aaron, 'Take a jar and put an omer of manna in it. Then place it before the LORD to be kept for the generations to come.' As the LORD commanded Moses, Aaron put the manna in front of the Testimony, that it might be kept."* The jar was not put in the ark, but it was placed in front of it to serve as a reminder. What about Aaron's staff? Numbers 17:10 says, *"The LORD said to Moses, 'Put back Aaron's staff in front of the Testimony, to be kept as a sign to the rebellious. This will put an end to their grumbling against me, so that they will not die.'"*

So Aaron's staff was also put in front of the ark, not in it. Even the Book of the Law was put outside of the ark.[27] Only the Ten Commandments were put in the ark. "Although the altar of incense stood in the Holy Place, the author describes it as belonging to the Most Holy Place. His purpose was to show its close relationship to the inner sanctuary and the ark of the covenant."[28] [Referring to Hebrews 9:3-4] I imagine the same is true with the author saying that the manna and staff were in the ark of the covenant. He just wanted to mention its close relationship with the ark of the covenant.

Leviticus 16:2, 13-15 says, *"The LORD said to Moses: 'Tell your brother Aaron not to come whenever he chooses into the Most Holy Place behind the curtain in front of the atonement cover on the ark, or else he will die, because I appear in the cloud over the atonement cover'...He is to put the incense on the fire before the LORD, and the smoke of the incense will conceal the atonement cover above the Testimony, so that he will not die. He is to take some of the bull's blood and with his finger sprinkle it on the front of the atonement cover; then he shall sprinkle some of it with his finger seven times before the atonement cover. He shall then slaughter the goat for the sin offering for the people and take its blood behind the curtain and do with it as he did with the bull's blood: He shall sprinkle it on the atonement cover and in front of it."*

Aaron, the high priest who God anointed, could not even go into the Most Holy Place whenever he wanted. He could only go in once a year to sacrifice for the sins of the people. God's presence dwelled between the two cherubim on the ark—that was an earthly copy of His Heavenly throne.

The cover over the ark was called the "atonement cover." This is the lid that enclosed the Ten Commandments in the ark. The Lord says, *"I appear in the cloud over the atonement cover on the ark."* This is a picture of God sitting on His throne. You can see why God's throne is called the Judgment seat. His throne contains the righteousness of the perfect law. The only way that Aaron and his descendants could go in was to bring incense in before them. Then they could sprinkle blood on and in front of the atonement cover, which brought forgiveness of sins for the people.

Where is the ark?

The ark of the covenant was never mentioned again after the Israelites were taken into exile into Babylon. It seems like they did not recover it as they built the second temple to the Lord. The ark was the heart and soul of their faith because it contained the Ten Commandments. The first temple was centered around the ark, as well as the law that was in it. It seems strange that if there actually would have been an ark for the second temple, it wasn't even mentioned at all. Maybe it was not mentioned because it is not needed anymore. In Jeremiah 3:16 it says, *"'In those days, when your numbers have increased greatly in the land,' declares the LORD, 'men will no longer say, 'The ark of the covenant of the LORD.' It will never enter their minds or be remembered; it will not be missed, nor will another one be made.'"* We know from the context of this passage, that it is talking about the time of the Messiah. When the Messiah comes we will no longer have need for the ark of the covenant. A priest no longer has to go into God's Presence to sacrifice for our sins. Our Messiah has come—Jesus offered Himself as a permanent sacrifice.

We don't have to seek out God's Presence in an inner room of a temple and sprinkle animal blood before His earthly throne (a copy of the real thing). No, Jesus' blood on the cross was the sacrifice needed before the heavenly throne of God.

I believe that we don't need the ark anymore, or God would have brought it back for us. 1 Samuel, chapters 4-6, talk about how the ark of the covenant was captured by the Philistines, and how God miraculously brought it back to the Israelites. If we still had a need for the law that was inside of it, God would have brought it back to us again. The time that the ark went missing is very interesting. Just as I said earlier, we have no record of it after Israel's exile to Babylon—that is the precise time that God told the people that He was going to make a new covenant with them. *"It will not be like the covenant I made with their forefathers* [law]...*I will put my law in their minds and write it on their hearts."*

Even though it appears as though the ark was not in the second temple built by Zerubbabel, God considered the second temple better than the first. God says the following about the second temple in Haggai 2:7,9, *"'I will shake all nations, and the desired of all nations will come, and I will fill this house with glory,' says the LORD Almighty... 'The glory of this present house will be greater than the glory of the former house,' says the LORD Almighty. 'And in this place I will grant peace,' declares the LORD Almighty."* We can only assume that God was saying the new temple has greater glory than the previous temple because Jesus Himself would be in the temple. The glory of the law in the Old Testament was no match for the glory that came in the person of Jesus Christ—God in flesh.

We can see how holy the ark of the covenant was.

2 Samuel 6: 6-7 says, *"When they came to the threshing floor of Nacon, Uzzah reached out and took hold of the ark of God, because the oxen stumbled. The LORD's anger burned against Uzzah because of his irreverent act; therefore God struck him down and he died there beside the ark of God."* No one could touch the ark and live, that is why they had poles to carry it with. No one can touch God's throne and expect to live. Can you imagine having to stand before such a holy place? In 2 Corinthians 5:10, Paul says that there will be a time when we will have to stand before God's holy throne. *"For we must all appear before the judgment seat of Christ, that each one may receive what is due him for the things done while in the body, whether good or bad."* That would be a terrifying place to be if we were going to be judged by the law. Fortunately for us, if we have made Jesus Christ our Lord and Savior, we know that His blood was sprinkled on the atonement cover in heaven on our behalf. We are not judged according to the law, but we are judged upon the righteousness of our Savior who died for us. Jesus was our substitution. He took our sin upon Himself, and we take on His righteousness. What a great trade, huh? But for those who have not clothed themselves with the righteousness of Christ, they will be judged on their own righteousness. That righteousness will get them the fire of hell for eternity. Clothe yourself in the blood of Jesus that is found in the new covenant relationship with Christ.

In Revelation we get one more glimpse of the ark of the covenant. Revelation 11:19 says, *"Then God's temple in heaven was opened, and within his temple was seen the ark of his covenant. And there came flashes of lightning, rumblings, peals of thunder, an earthquake and a great hailstorm."* When God's temple is opened up in heaven, we see the ark of the covenant...We see God's heavenly throne. When we reach that point, it will be too late to decide to live in a covenant relationship with God. We will be judged by the decisions we made here on earth.

In the old covenant, they were judged according to the law and they had to bring a sacrifice each year to atone for their sins. In the new covenant we are not judged by the law. It all boils down to whether or not you have your name written in the Lamb's Book of Life. If not, the righteous Judge, who sits on the throne, will see that there is no atonement for your sins.

Chapter 10

Sacred Days In The Church

In Leviticus 23 there is a list of all of the festivals and sacred days that Israel had to observe according to the Law of Moses. In this chapter, I want to give you a brief description of those sacred days and how Christ fulfilled them, or will fulfill them in His second coming. Christ's fulfillment of these Jewish sacred days became sacred days for the church.

Passover

The Passover was the first festival of the year. Israel was supposed to observe Passover every year on the fourteenth day of the first month. They did this to remember how God brought them out of Egypt, out of the land of slavery. In Exodus 12, we read about the Passover story. The Lord says to the Israelites in verse 7, *"Go kill a lamb and smear its blood over the doorframe of your houses."* This seems to be an odd request. "You want me to get blood and smear it around my door?" But after seeing the nine amazing plagues that God performed in Egypt, I am sure it was quite easy for the people to obey this particular instruction. God outlines exactly what will happen for the Israelites. For the houses that have the blood around their doors, the firstborn will not die. However, the houses that do not have the blood around the door, the firstborn will be struck down. Exodus 12:23 says, *"When the Lord goes through the land to strike down the Egyptians, he will see the blood on the top and sides of the doorframe and will pass over that doorway, and he will not permit the destroyer to enter your houses and strike you down."* In Psalms 78, the agent of God's wrath against the Egyptians is described as "a band of destroying angels". So these destroying angels were sent to kill the firstborn of every household. The blood was the sign that the angels were looking for. The sign wasn't a particular style of house, or how big the house was; not even the kind of door or door knob on the house, or whether it was an Egyptian home or Israelite home. The only distinctive mark the angels were looking for was blood around the door. If some of the Israelites would have rejected God and not put the blood around their doors thinking, "Oh this is silly. I'm not going to do that!" Their firstborn would have died. I imagine if the Egyptians would have received word of what was happening, and put blood around their doors, their firstborn would have lived. The destroyer didn't stop and look around at the situation and make decisions. It was clear cut for them—was the doorframe covered with blood or not? If so, it would pass by, and the firstborn in that house was saved. Nothing but the blood saved them. I hope we see the importance of the blood in the Passover event.

It was the blood that saved them, but it couldn't be just any blood. They couldn't go out and kill a cow and put its blood on the door frame. We see in Exodus 12:5 that God says**,** *"The animals you choose must be year-old males without defect and you may take them from the sheep or the goats."* The Lord is getting very specific. It has to be a lamb without defect. God didn't want them to pick a sickly animal and sacrifice it to Him. God wanted the best. They also received instructions in

Exodus 12:46, *"Do not break any of the bones."* None of the bones of the Passover lamb were to be broken. It is interesting to compare these verses with Jesus. All of these things that the Israelites had to do during the Passover actually parallel Jesus as our New Passover lamb. When Jesus was on the cross, the soldiers came and broke the legs of both the criminals that were hanging next to Jesus because they wanted to kill them quicker. But when they came to Jesus, He was already dead so they didn't break his legs. No bones were broken on our Passover lamb.

Jesus was also our perfect lamb without defect. Jesus was perfect. He never sinned. 1 Peter 1:18-19 says, *"For you know that it was not with perishable things such as silver or gold that you were redeemed from your empty way of life handed down to you from your forefathers, but with the precious blood of Christ, a lamb without blemish or defect."*

Jesus is our Passover lamb who was sacrificed. It is His blood that we put over the doorframes of our lives. When it comes time for judgment, God is not going to look at our ethnic background, or how rich or poor we were. He doesn't look at how smart we are, or where we worked. He is going to look at one thing—are we covered by the blood of the Lamb? The lamb's blood saved the Israelites from slavery in Egypt, but the blood of Jesus saves us from eternal punishment for our sins.

Unleavened Bread

The Festival of Unleavened Bread is tied together with the Passover feast. It happens every year on the fifteenth through the twenty first of the first month. This Festival is a remembrance of how the Israelites had to leave Egypt hastily. They didn't even have time to let the yeast rise in their bread. Exodus 12:39 says, *"With the dough they had brought from Egypt, they baked cakes of unleavened bread. The dough was without yeast because they had been driven out of Egypt and did not have time to prepare food for themselves."* They left Egypt as quickly as they could. So at this festival, they were not supposed to eat any yeast as a reminder of God's deliverance.

Yeast in the Bible is often thought of as being evil or corrupt. Jesus says in Mark 8:15, *"...Watch out for the yeast of the Pharisees and that of Herod."* The corrupt teachings of these people are like yeast, all you need is a little and it will spread out of control. Don't get caught up in false teaching and be led astray. Jesus' death on the cross was the death to sin. Jesus permanently removed the yeast (sin) from us.

Paul talks about yeast in 1 Corinthians 5:6-8, which says, *"Your boasting is not good. Don't you know that a little yeast works through the whole batch of dough? Get rid of the old yeast that you may be a new batch without yeast—as you really are. For Christ, our Passover lamb, has been sacrificed. Therefore let us keep the Festival, not with the old yeast, the yeast of malice and wickedness, but with bread without yeast, the bread of sincerity and truth."* We are to continue to remember the festival, but not in the old way by eating bread without yeast, but in the new way of ridding the sin from our lives. We are to get rid of the yeast (sin), and live our lives for God. A little sin in our lives has a great impact on all of the areas of our lives. Just like dying to sin (getting rid of the yeast), has a huge positive impact on our entire lives.

Firstfruits

The Firstfruits was a sacred day held on the sixteenth of the first month—two days after the Passover Festival. Leviticus 23:9-10 says, *"The LORD said to Moses, 'Speak to the Israelites and say to them: 'When you enter the land I am going to give you and you reap its harvest, bring to the priest a sheaf of the first grain you harvest.'"* This was a festival recognizing the Lord's bounty in the upcoming harvest. The Israelites would bring the very firstfruits to the Lord, with a great expectation of more harvest to come.

Paul talks about the firstfruits in 1 Corinthians 15. In verse 20 he says, *"But Christ has indeed been raised from the dead, the firstfruits of those who have fallen asleep."* This verse is referring back to this Leviticus passage. Paul makes an analogy between Christ's resurrection and the Old Testament ritual of firstfruits giving. The firstfruits were the very first portions of the harvest, and they were given to God as an offering. The firstfruits were an indication that the entire harvest was soon to follow. The firstfruits were not the end of the harvest; there was much more to come. Verse 23 goes on to talk about the resurrection, *"But each in his own turn: Christ, the firstfruits; then, when he comes, those who belong to him."* In Paul's view, Christ's resurrection was not an isolated event. It represents the beginning of something larger. His resurrection promised the rest of the harvest will come soon (which is the resurrection of the believers). Paul's logic to the people was that Christ first rose from the dead, and that He is the firstfruits offered to God. Then the rest of the harvest will come, which is our resurrection. Christ's resurrection was more than one person's triumph over death, it was a sign that all believers would triumph over death.

The Firstfruits Festival was fulfilled when Jesus rose from the dead. Jesus died on a Friday (Passover), and He rose from the dead two days later (Sunday—on the third day).

Feast of Weeks

The Feast of Weeks was a festival after the harvest recognizing the Lord's goodness. It was a time to be thankful for all that the Lord provides. It took place in the third month on the sixth day. Leviticus 23:16 says, *"Count off fifty days up to the day after the seventh Sabbath, and then present an offering of new grain to the LORD."* The Feast of Weeks was fifty days after the seventh Sabbath, which was the Sabbath after the Passover celebration. We see in the New Testament, after Jesus' death, that the disciples met together on the "Feast of Weeks" (which was called Pentecost—meaning fifty). Acts 2:1 says, *"When the day of Pentecost came, they were all together in one place."* It was the first day of the week, and God's Spirit came down upon the disciples in power. They were able to speak in tongues (I will explain the significance of that later) and the people stood amazed at what they heard. They saw this new amazing way that God was working in their midst.

We see God working a little differently in the new covenant, than how He had worked in the old covenant. Exodus 19:1 says, *"In the third month after the Israelites left Egypt—on the very day—they came to the Desert of Sinai."* Exodus 19 was in the third month, the same year that they left Egypt. So it is the same time frame when Israel would (in the future) gather for the Feast of Weeks (sixth day of the third month). It was in Exodus 20 where God gives the Israelites the Ten Commandments to follow. So it is very possible that the Law in the Old

Testament and the Spirit in the New Testament were given on the same day.

Remember when Moses received the law of the Ten Commandments from the Lord? He came down and saw the people worshipping the golden calf and he threw down the Ten Commandments and broke them. Moses commanded Aaron to have the Levites go through the camp and kill his brother, friend and neighbor. Then, in Exodus 32:28 it says, *"The Levites did as Moses commanded, and that day about three thousand of the people died."* Jump ahead to the New Testament when the disciples received the Spirit. The Jews came to Jerusalem for the sacred assembly over Pentecost. There were many God fearing Jews all over the known world because of the Assyrian invasion of Israel and the Babylonian exile of Judah. Many of the Jews were faithful, and would still come back and celebrate this Holy Festival. There were many Jews in Jerusalem on this Pentecost festival, representing many languages all over the world. When the Spirit came down upon the disciples, they began to speak in many other languages that they had never had studied before. They accomplished this with the power of the Holy Spirit. The Jews from other lands, who came to hear the Old Testament teachings that they heard many times before, heard for the first time the gospel message of Jesus Christ, and it was proclaimed in their own language. They heard how the Messiah came and died on the cross for their sins. Peter preached to the crowd and it says in Acts 2:41, *"Those who accepted his message were baptized, and about three thousand were added to their number that day."* The old and new covenants both had a grand opening celebration. One brought death to three thousand and the other brought eternal life through the Spirit to three thousand.

The Feast of Weeks was a time of thanksgiving to God for all of His provisions. In the New Testament it became known as Pentecost, a time of thanksgiving for the Spirit that He put inside of us to live for Him.

Unfulfilled Festivals

These festivals will only be fulfilled when Christ is ready to return and does return. It is so much easier to write about the festivals that have been fulfilled because you can point to the Bible verses where Jesus fulfilled them. But when it hasn't happened yet, it is much more difficult to interpret what exactly will happen in the future. We know the final result—Satan is put away and we will live eternally with our Savior. However, the details of that victory are only a guess. There are many people out there who have their own opinions on how it will happen, and they believe everyone else is wrong. That is not me. As I write about the future fulfillment of Christ's return, these are the opinions that I have at this time. God may give me new insights that I do not have at this time. My main concern in writing this chapter is for people to see that Jesus did fulfill the feasts above, and how He will one day fulfill the festivals below in the way He chooses!

In the Jewish calendar, the following three feasts were close together. They were all in the seventh month. The Feast of Trumpets was held on the first day of the month. The Day of Atonement was observed on the tenth day of the month. And finally the Feast of Tabernacles started on the fifteenth day of the month and went through the twenty-first. These festivals happened one right after another with very little time between them. As we look at these future fulfillments, there is not much time, if any, from one to the other.

The Feast of Trumpets

The Feast of Trumpets is one that we don't hear much about in scripture. The feast took place on the first day of the seventh month. It is referenced four times in scripture: Leviticus 23:23, Numbers 29:1, Ezra 3:6, and Nehemiah 8:2. None of these scriptures seem to give us a good understanding of what this festival is all about. We know it was a day the people were to present themselves before the Lord and hear the trumpets being sounded. More than likely it was a call for the people to repent of their way of life. The Festival of Trumpets was only 9 days before the Day of Atonement, where the priest would go into the Most Holy Place to sacrifice a lamb for our sins. Trumpet calls were often used to convey the message, "Get yourself ready!" Whether it was for battle, for a coming king, or for worship, they needed to be prepared!

The word trumpets in this festival is plural, so it seems to be referring to the seven trumpets we read about in Revelation. The angels blew the trumpets in Revelation to bring about catastrophes on the earth so that people would repent before the coming King of Kings. It says in Revelation 9:20-21 after the sixth trumpet sound, *"The rest of mankind that were not killed by these plagues still did not repent of the work of their hands; they did not stop worshiping demons, and idols of gold, silver, bronze, stone and wood—idols that cannot see or hear or walk. Nor did they repent of their murders, their magic arts, their sexual immorality or their thefts."* These people are not getting themselves ready for when Jesus comes to bring justice to the earth. The trumpets have sounded to warn them, but they still choose to live in rebellion.

It is easy to look around at our world and see all

of the catastrophes that have occurred over the last many years. Wars are all over the globe, natural disasters are taking thousands and thousands of lives, and diseases are taking hundreds of thousands of lives. Could God be waking up our world today saying, "My coming is close! Be prepared! Repent and come to me now!"

When the seventh trumpet sounds, repentance will be too late. It says in Revelation 11:15, *"The seventh angel sounded his trumpet, and there were loud voices in heaven, which said: 'The kingdom of the world has become the kingdom of our Lord and of his Christ, and he will reign for ever and ever.'"* What a great day that will be for those who have repented of their sinful lives before the coming of the King! This ushers in the Atonement Day.

Atonement Day

Atonement Day was probably the biggest day on the Jewish calendar. It was celebrated on the tenth day of the seventh month closely following the Feast of Trumpets. There is something interesting as you look at the Day of Atonement in Leviticus 16. Aaron (or the high priest) was to sacrifice a goat for the sins of the people and take the blood and sprinkle it in the Most Holy place on the Atonement cover, but there was another goat that was a part of the process. Leviticus 16:20-22 says, *"When Aaron has finished making atonement for the Most Holy Place, the Tent of Meeting and the altar, he shall bring forward the live goat. He is to lay both hands on the head of the live goat and confess over it all the wickedness and rebellion of the Israelites—all their sins—and put them on the goat's head. He shall send the goat away into the desert in the care of a man appointed for the task. The goat will carry on itself all their sins to a solitary place;*

and the man shall release it in the desert." We know that Jesus represents the goat that died for us—it was His blood that saved us. This passage says that there is also a live goat that will carry all of the sins of the people and will be led by a man to be taken to a solitary place. Jesus is the one who died for our sins, so who represents the live goat that will carry away the sins of the people to a solitary place? There seems to be a good comparison of that in Revelation 20:1-3. Which says, *"And I saw an angel coming down out of heaven, having the key to the Abyss and holding in his hand a great chain. He seized the dragon, that ancient serpent, who is the devil, or Satan, and bound him for a thousand years. He threw him into the Abyss, and locked and sealed it over him, to keep him from deceiving the nations anymore until the thousand years were ended. After that, he must be set free for a short time."* The angel will lead Satan into the Abyss, and Satan will be getting the full wrath of God.

Atonement Day in the Old Testament was a day when the high priest would sacrifice for his sins and for the sins of the people. Their sins would be atoned for, for a year, but the next year the high priest would have to do it all over again. When our High Priest from heaven returns, sin will be completely done away with. We will be perfect, as God created us to be. Sin will be gone forever, placed upon Satan and gone into the great Abyss.

The Feast of Tabernacles

The Feast of Tabernacles was celebrated five days after the Day of Atonement, from the fifteenth through the twenty first of the seventh month. This was a weeklong festival to remember the journey that the Israelites took from Egypt to the Promise Land. During the festival they would live in booths to remind them of their lives in the desert, and they would recall how God led them safely to the land that He promised them.

The Feast of Tabernacles points to the Great Wedding Banquet of God. "A Jewish wedding in Biblical times would have a feast that could last a week."[29] In Luke 14, there is a parable about a Great Wedding Banquet. The parable came about because of something that a man in the crowd said in verse 15. *"Blessed is the man who will eat at the feast in the kingdom of God."* This man is dreaming about how good it will be. Happy will be the day when we are feasting with the Lord in His kingdom. Yes indeed, that will be a great day! It is like a victory supper. I have played on a lot of sports teams, and after we have won a tournament or something similar—to sit around the table with your teammates and eat—what a great time that is! We would be laughing and talking about the great plays that were made. For example, during my senior year in high school, our basketball team made it to the state tournament. On the way to state we beat the #1 ranked team in the state. That night we talked of nothing else. We were remembering key plays and how we came back from behind and did the impossible. We had an amazing time of fellowship, and recalling the victory with our teammates. But when we sit with our Lord to celebrate the victory that we will have claimed here on earth, through the power of His Spirit—that will be a million times better! We will sit with fellow believers and celebrate that we didn't give up, but kept the faith even in the difficult times. We will remember the journey of our lives that brought us to the Promise Land. I want to be one of those people who sit at that table during the victory feast of God.

I remember as I was growing up, our family would get together at Grandpa and Grandma Litwiller's house for Christmas. All of my aunts, uncles and cousins were there. There were way too many people there to sit at one table. So they had a grown-up table, and they had a table for the kids in another room. I have always remembered that I wanted so desperately to sit at the grown-up table. One day I made it to the grown-up table and I was so happy. What a great day that was! But as good as that was for me, the grown-up table is nothing compared to our Father's table that we will get to enjoy in heaven. What a day that will be!

The Feast of Tabernacles was also known as the Feast of Ingathering. People would gather together to give thanks to God for His blessings that He gave them in this Promise Land of Canaan. In the days ahead, we believers will be gathered in and we will be giving thanks to God for the provisions of the Promise Land of Heaven. Luke 13:29 says, *"People will come from east and west and north and south, and will take their places at the feast in the kingdom of God."* We will be gathered from every nation, tribe and tongue as we give thanks and remember the victories of our journey that God brought us through.

Chapter 11

Living Under The New Covenant

If I am not under the law, does that mean I don't have to tithe to go to heaven? Do I need to be baptized to go to heaven? Do I need to go to church to go to heaven? Do I have to live a sexually pure life to go to heaven? Often, these questions are asked because it is something we don't want to do. You might say, "I don't want to give up 10% of my money to God, I don't feel the need to be baptized, or I don't want to waste a couple hours of my life each week going to church. I don't even want to live sexually pure in this impure world." All of these questions that people ask can basically be summed up by saying: "What is the least amount I can do and yet still go to heaven? I want to go to heaven, but I don't want to give up any more than I have to. I want to follow God, but I don't want it to change my lifestyle."

The danger with people figuring out this truth that they are not under the law any more, is that they now believe that there is no standard to live by. "I am free from the law, so I don't have to live by any standards." Paul addresses this kind of thinking in Ephesians 6:15-16. *"What then? Shall we sin because we are not under law but under grace? By no means! Don't you know that when you offer yourselves to someone to obey him as slaves, you are slaves to the one whom you obey— whether you are slaves to sin, which leads to death, or to obedience, which leads to righteousness?"* Paul is writing to this church because of all of the false teachings that were being taught. Many people believed that they could keep sinning, which would lead to more grace. Paul vehemently denies that. You are on the wrong path if you think that you can continue to sin because you are not under the law.

    We not only see this kind of thinking in Biblical times. We see it throughout all of history. The Early Church was on fire for the Lord and they lived sold out devoted lives to Jesus. But as centuries passed, the same commitment was not found in the church. There came a time in the church when it became all about works. The people lived however they wanted to live, and they would come to church once a week and pay indulgences and confess their sins to the priest to have their sins forgiven. It was all about works. Martin Luther saw the error in that way of thinking and he broke off from the church. He brought reformation. He said, "It is only by grace we are saved." Unfortunately the pendulum swung the other direction. People began to say, "I am saved by grace; it is by nothing that I do. So I will accept Jesus as my Savior and then I can go live however I want." They believed this passage meant that they were no longer under law, and that they could do whatever they wanted. After Martin Luther, came the Anabaptist movement. They agreed with Martin Luther that "it is only by grace we are saved", but also said that works are evidence of your salvation. If you have truly received the grace of God in your lives, God's grace will change the way that you live your life. You won't want to live an unholy life that is in rebellion to the law.

Anabaptists believe that we are free from the law, but not free to live unholy lives. We would shout "Amen" to Paul's statement in Galatians 5:13, when he says, *"You, my brothers, were called to be free. But do not use your freedom to indulge in the sinful nature; rather serve one another in love."* We are free from the law, but we are not free to continue to follow our sinful nature. I want to follow the leading of God's Spirit in me, not the self serving desires of my flesh.

It is naive to think that Jesus came to die upon the cross so that we can continue to live our sinful lives. The problem is that people still teach that we can live however we choose because Jesus' sacrifice on the cross will forgive them. We were warned about that kind of teaching in the Bible. Jude 4 says, *"For certain men whose condemnation was written about long ago, have secretly slipped in among you. They are godless men, who change the grace of our God into a license for immorality and deny Jesus Christ our only Sovereign and Lord."* Jesus' cross, His fulfillment of the law, doesn't give us permission to live like the devil. Jesus' blood purchased the salvation of those who are in a committed relationship with Him.

Works accompany faith

James 2 illustrates the impossibility of us saying we have faith, yet at the same time, having no works in our lives to show for our faith.

> *[14] What good is it, my brothers, if a man claims to have faith but has no deeds? Can such faith save him? [15] Suppose a brother or sister is without clothes and daily food. [16] If one of you*

says to him, "Go, I wish you well; keep warm and well fed," but does nothing about his physical needs, what good is it? [17] *In the same way, faith by itself, if it is not accompanied by action, is dead.*

[18] *But someone will say, "You have faith; I have deeds."*

Show me your faith without deeds, and I will show you my faith by what I do. [19] *You believe that there is one God. Good! Even the demons believe that—and shudder.*

[20] *You foolish man, do you want evidence that faith without deeds is useless?* [21] *Was not our ancestor Abraham considered righteous for what he did when he offered his son Isaac on the altar?* [22] *You see that his faith and his actions were working together, and his faith was made complete by what he did.* [23] *And the scripture was fulfilled that says, "Abraham believed God, and it was credited to him as righteousness," and he was called God's friend.* [24] *You see that a person is justified by what he does and not by faith alone.* [25] *In the same way, was not even Rahab the prostitute considered righteous for what she did when she gave lodging to the spies and sent*

> *them off in a different direction? ^{26} As the body without the spirit is dead, so faith without deeds is dead.*

Our lives need to match what we believe. Picture with me a husband who says, "I love my wife," yet he verbally and physically abuses her, he is unfaithful to her, and is totally unwilling to sacrifice anything to make his wife happy. Does he really love his wife? I say no way! These are just words. If he truly loved his wife, his actions would be different. He would stop yelling at her, stop beating her, he would be faithful to her alone, and he would be willing to reprioritize his life to make her happy. Our actions do match what we truly believe! If they don't, we don't believe in it strongly enough to change our behaviors. James says in verse 19, *"You believe that there is one God. Good! Even the demons believe that—and shudder."* It is not enough to confess it with your lips that Jesus is Lord. You have to truly believe it with your heart and it will change the way that you live your life. It will not just be head knowledge that Jesus is Lord, but it will be a surrendering of the way you live your life.

I heard a sermon illustration one time that talked about how we need to have both faith and works working together. Suppose you are on a row boat, and you have two oars. One oar we will name "faith", the other oar we will name "works". What happens when you just paddle with faith? You go around in circles. What happens when you just paddle with works? The same is true, you go around in circles. But when you use both faith and works together, what happens? You move the boat forward towards your desired destination. In the Christian life you cannot separate faith and works. They are both needed.

The thing is, when we accept Jesus into our lives, we don't want to live the same old lives that we have been living….everything changes. We become new in Christ Jesus. 2 Corinthians 5:17 says, *"Therefore, if anyone is in Christ, he is a new creation; the old has gone, and the new has come!"* We are new creations…we are not the same self centered people that we were before we accepted Christ. We should now say, "Life used to be all about me, and now it is all about God." We have been made new because we have replaced our sinful nature with the Spirit of the Holy God. God's Spirit inside of us completely changes our attitudes and our behaviors. In Ephesians 4:1 Paul says, *"As a prisoner for the Lord, then, I urge you to live a life worthy of the calling you have received."* We have all received a calling from God to live for Him. When He becomes Lord of our lives, He expects us to live a certain way. He wants us to enter into a covenant relationship with Him.

In my first book, Living out the Called Life, there is a chapter about covenant relationships. I would like to share some of the main points that I thought were important in that book throughout the rest of this chapter. A covenant is an agreement between two parties. Your marriage is a covenant relationship. You both agree to love, honor, and be faithful to each other as long as you both shall live. This marriage relationship is completely different than all of our other relationships. Your spouse is your helpmate for life. We may have good neighbors and good friends but we don't have that same level of commitment with them as we do with our spouse. We don't have a covenant relationship with our neighbors.

We will help them if we can…and who knows? In the future, we may move far away from them and get new neighbors. But in our covenant walk with our spouse, we are committed to them for life.

Too often we treat our relationship with God like He is a good friend or neighbor. We treat Him like any other relationship that we have. But our relationship with God should be a covenant relationship. Our baptism is like our wedding day to God. When we are baptized it is like we say to God, "I love you, and at this moment I vow to follow and be faithful to you for the rest of my life." We know that a marriage will only be good if both people live out their part of the covenant agreement. If your spouse is only looking out for their own best interest, the marriage will not be a good one.

Janelle and I just made this covenant vow to each other not too long ago. I vowed to spend the rest of my life with her…to love her, cherish her, and put no one ahead of her, to be faithful to her as long as we both shall live. What if, in our counseling, as she was sitting beside me, I made this comment to the preacher marrying us, saying, "What is the least amount I need to do, and yet still be married to her? Do I have to show an interest in the things she does? Do I have to provide for her? Does she have to be my top priority other than God?" How do you think that would go over with Janelle? Not good, and understandably so. I am still expecting her to meet her marital obligations to me, and be my helpmate…but in return, I would be trying to do as little as possible for her. It would be as though I want to be married, but I wouldn't want to give anything up. I would want all that she has to offer me, but I couldn't possibly make the same sacrifices back to her. You see, I would only want the blessings of married life; I wouldn't want to put in all of the work required. Would you want to be in that kind of a relationship with this type of person? No way!

Unfortunately, that is how most of us enter into our relationship with Jesus. We want the covenant blessings, but we don't want to live out our part of the covenant agreement. We want the eternal life that He has to offer. We want His love, His peace, His guidance, His protection, and we want His provisions. We want all of the blessings from God, but we don't want to do much of anything in return. We want and expect God to keep His part of the agreement, but we are very passive about actually living out our part. We think to ourselves, God is merciful, so I don't need to live out my part. That is a lie from the devil. We have a tendency to think that we can be the same unchanged people that we have always been, and that we don't need to change anything because Jesus will forgive us anyway. God is merciful, but that does not mean that we keep on living a selfish and sinful life. He died to forgive our sins, not to allow us to keep on living for ourselves.

I'm not questioning whether anyone has a relationship with Jesus or not. I believe you all have a relationship with Jesus if you are reading this book. But the question is: Do you have a covenant relationship with Jesus? Or is He like the neighbor next door whom you contact only when you need help. God demands more than that. In Matthew 7:21-23 Jesus says, *"Not everyone who says to me, 'Lord, Lord,' will enter the kingdom of heaven, but only he who does the will of my Father who is in heaven. Many will say to me on that day, 'Lord, Lord, did we not prophesy in your name, and in your name drive out demons and perform many miracles?' Then I will tell them plainly, 'I never knew you. Away from me, you evildoers!'"* This passage shows there are people who believe that they are going to heaven, but they are not. They thought that they knew Jesus, but Jesus tells them, "I never knew you." You were not in a covenant relationship with Him.

      Again, our relationship with God should be like the relationship that you have with your spouse. It is a daily walk in good times and in the times where it becomes a real sacrifice to fulfill your covenant obligations. Just like in your marriage, it is not always easy to live for God. But it is definitely worth it. Stop and think about who is getting the better end of the deal in our relationship with God. If you look at all that God offers in His part of the covenant, compared to what we need to do in our part of the covenant…we are really getting a great deal. We have the power of the Holy Spirit in our earthly lives, and we have an eternal life in heaven waiting for us. God treats us like His favorite son or daughter. You are the apple of His eye.

      Our lives should be lived in response to the mercy that Jesus showed us on the cross. We all get to choose how we want to live our lives…God will not force you to live in a covenant relationship with Him, but it would be a mistake not to. Hebrews 10:28-31 says, *"Anyone who rejected the law of Moses died without mercy on the testimony of two or three witnesses. How much more severely do you think a man deserves to be punished who has trampled the Son of God under foot, who has treated as an unholy thing the blood of the covenant that sanctified him, and who has insulted the Spirit of grace? For we know him who said, 'It is mine to avenge; I will repay,' and again, 'The Lord will judge his people.' It is a dreadful thing to fall into the hands of the living God."* Under the old covenant people were killed for their rebellion against God in the law, but in the new covenant, people will be thrown into eternal punishment for their rejection of the blood that was shed for them. How dreadful it is to fall into the hands of the living God! God won't force you to forgive someone, or to live sexually pure lives, or to tithe. It is up to you to decide if you want this kind of relationship with God. But let me say, there is nothing more important to me than my relationship with Jesus. Nothing! I hope you feel the same way.

    As you contemplate how you choose to live in this new covenant relationship, let me leave you with the words Paul shares in Galatians 6:7-9, *"Do not be deceived: God cannot be mocked. A man reaps what he sows. The one who sows to please his sinful nature, from that nature will reap destruction; the one who sows to please the Spirit, from the Spirit will reap eternal life. Let us not become weary in doing good, for at the proper time we will reap a harvest if we do not give up."*

Conclusion

I am thankful for the Holy Word of God. Every word in the Bible is God-breathed[30] and is useful in our walk in this world. The Old Testament gives us great stories of faith, and it helps us understand how God worked with His people in the past. It is a solid foundation that the New Testament is built upon. I could not imagine not having the Old Testament to read because it helps me to know God in greater detail.

    I am also thankful that I am not under the yoke of the law found in the Old Testament writings. I just read Exodus, Leviticus, Numbers and Deuteronomy this week—and I am so thankful that I am not under these regulations in the law! Jesus Christ came to save me and to release me to live by the Spirit whom He put inside of me. Jesus did not come for us to live in opposition to the law, but to fulfill it and to bring the law to its intentional goal. We are no longer supposed to simply keep the external criteria of the law, but we are to follow the character in which the law was given. The old covenant was set up to institute external behaviors such as do not murder or commit adultery, but the new covenant was instituted to work on our hearts and attitudes. It teaches us that we should not lust or carry anger in our hearts. Jesus told us in Matthew 23:26, *"...First clean the inside of the cup and dish, and then the outside also will be clean."* If we clean our hearts and attitudes, our outward behaviors will follow suit. As Christians, we still follow the Old Testament writings, but we must look at them through the backdrop of the new covenant that Jesus instituted.

It would be wrong for any of us to assume that since we are not under the law, that there is no standard of living that we have to follow. People who believe that in their hearts are truly not in a covenant walk with the Lord. Hear the Apostle Paul's plea in Galatians 5:13, *"You, my brothers, were called to be free. But do not use your freedom to indulge in the sinful nature; rather, serve one another in love."* We should not take the freedom that Christ gives us for granted. The grace that Jesus so freely gave us should motivate us to live our lives in a pleasing way to Him.

Thank you for taking this journey with me. I cannot finish without giving everyone an opportunity to know that they can be saved through the precious blood of our Savior—not through your good deeds. If you repent and confess your sins, you can know without a shadow of a doubt that God will wash them away. My friends, if you enter into this new covenant relationship with Jesus, you do not need to worry about your eternal rest. Romans 8:1 says, *"Therefore, there is now no condemnation for those who are in Christ Jesus."* Let the meaning of that verse comfort your spirit. If you are in this new covenant with God through Christ Jesus, there is no condemnation. You are saved by the righteousness of the One who died for you! Please pray with me.

Lord,
I thank you for your Holy Word that You have given me so that I can know You. Without it, I wouldn't know about Your

great love for me. I confess to you right now that I am a sinner. You saw my hopeless estate, that there was no way that I could make it to heaven by my own goodness. There was no way that I could keep the holy standards that you set up in your law. You desired a relationship with me so much, that You willingly came down and took the cruel, cruel cross for me. Lord you freed me from death's grip. I confess right now that I want to die to myself, so that I can live in you. I know that as I lay my life before your altar, You have freed me to serve you through the Spirit found in the new covenant. Thank you that I am no longer under the law that is powerless to save me. In Jesus' name, Amen.

References

[1] NIV Study Bible, p. 150.
[2] NIV Study Bible, p. 176.
[3] NIV Study Bible, p. 1870; Footnote to Hebrews 10:19.
[4] There are some Christian fellowships such as Seventh Day Adventist that still hold to the Jewish Sabbath Day.
[5] There are some Christian fellowships such as Seventh Day Adventist that still hold to the Dietary Law.
[6] William Wimmer, pastor of Grace Chapel Church of God, Benton, Arkansas "preachingtoday.com"
[7] Matthew 27:51.
[8] NIV Study Bible. p. 1572; Footnote Luke 16:16.
[9] NIV Study Bible. p. 1450; Footnote Matthew 5:21.
[10] Scot McKnight, The NIV Application Commentary: Galatians (Zondervan 1995), p. 184.
[11] www.sermonnotebook.org MARRIED? YES! BUT, TO WHICH HUSBAND? Romans 7:1-6.
[12] Romans 5:12-21.
[13] www.sermonnotebook.org MARRIED? YES! BUT, TO WHICH HUSBAND? Romans 7:1-6.
[14] Galatians 3:1.
[15] http://jeffvoegtlin.wordpress.com/2006/09/11/abba-father-galatians-41-7-2/
[16] Romans 4:17
[17] http://www.kaleochurch.com/sermon/galatians-421-31/
[18] http://www.freegrace.net/Sermon/Genesis_16.htm
[19] I always relate the Sanhedrin to the United States Congress, which is made up of Democrats and Republicans, which hold strongly to different beliefs. Sanhedrin is made up of Sadducees and Pharisees, which have some sharp disagreements.
[20] NIV Study Bible, p. 1519; Footnote to Mark 12:28.
[21] Walvoord, John F., and Zuck, Roy B., *The Bible Knowledge Commentary*, (Wheaton, Illinois: Scripture Press Publications, Inc.) 1983, 1985.
[22] NIV Study Bible, p. 1875, Footnote Hebrews 12:18-21.
[23] Romans 2:28-29.
[24] 1 Sam 4:4, 1 Sam 6:2, 2 Kings 19:15, 1 Chronicles 13:6, Psalm 80:1, Psalm 99:1
[25] Also says the same thing in 2 Chronicles 5:10
[26] Deuteronomy 31:24-26
[27] NIV Study Bible, p. 1868, Footnote Hebrews 9:4
[28] NIV Study Bible, p. 1595, Footnote John 2:1
[29] 2 Timothy 3:16.

About The Author

Kurt Litwiller has been the head pastor at Boynton Mennonite Church in Hopedale, Illinois, since April of 2001. He graduated with a Master's of Divinity degree from Lincoln Christian Seminary in December of 2001. He also holds a Sports Management degree from Goshen College in Indiana (1995) and a Liberal Arts degree from Hesston College in Kansas (1993). He married his wife Janelle in the summer of 2008, and they enjoy impacting lives together for the kingdom of God in their little town of Hopedale.

Need additional copies?

To order more copies of
New Covenant Living,
contact NewBookPublishing.com

- ❏ Order online at NewBookPublishing.com
- ❏ Call 877-311-5100 or
- ❏ Email Info@NewBookPublishing.com

Call for multiple copy discounts!

Reliance Media

Another book by Kurt Litwiller:

Living Out The Called Life
Running God's Race

Many people say they believe in God, but does that truly change the way they live their lives? Some people today say they are a Christian, but they do not act like one. Once we receive Jesus Christ as our Lord, we are called to live a certain way. In Ephesians 4:1, Paul says, *"...live a life worthy of the calling you have received."* We cannot continue to live for ourselves and gratify our sinful natures—we need to live sold out lives for God instead! The Bible talks often about how our life is a race. If you want to win the prize, you need to persevere in tough times and compete by the rules. God's Word tells us how we should run our race here on this earth. We need to run God's race if we want to receive the reward that God has for us.

To order copies of
Living Out The Called Life,
contact NewBookPublishing.com

- ❐ Order online at NewBookPublishing.com
- ❐ Call 877-311-5100 or
- ❐ Email Info@NewBookPublishing.com